THE ULTIMATE KINDLE MARKETING GUIDE

The Best Collection of Marketing Tactics to Boost Your Sales

TIMO Hofstee

Copyright 2014

Update 2022

Contents

Copyright

Introduction

Congratulations! You have your book ready to publish it on Amazon. Now you just go onto Amazon, submit your book and wait a couple of hours before it is live on Amazon.

And then you can sit back and just have to wait till big piles of money fill up your bank account in no time!

If you think that that's the way it works, then I really have to disappoint you. And I don't really understand why you have bought my book.

Attention: BIG SPOILER AHEAD!

Unless you are Stephen King or JK Rowling, this is NOT the way it works. (In case that you are one of these authors: I'm honored that you read my eBook. Can you please leave me a review? Thank you).

No, I didn't know it either. When I published my first eBook on Amazon, I hit publish and waited. And nothing happened. Hmm, what's wrong?

Well, this is similar as opening a hamburger shop at the end of a dead end in an outskirt without any signage outdoor and no ads in the newspaper.

What's wrong with that is: If people cannot find what you're selling, then they also cannot buy it. It's as simple as that. And that's what we call "marketing".

And that's what this book is all about. How do you market your book? Where can you find your audience? How should you price it? How do you promote it on social media? How to follow your sales? How to use special deals and promotions? What keywords to use? What categories?

The difference between marketing your book and NOT marketing your book will make a big difference. And especially if you're a starting indie writer.

Notice that marketing your book will NOT guarantee you any sure success. That's because something like sure success doesn't exist. I cannot tell if your book is a potential killer or not. No one can. People with a lot of experience in publishing MIGHT have an idea if your book has potential or not.

But do you know how many titles have been published in paper over the last century and were taken out of the bookshops after a couple of weeks to make place for other titles?

Most of them. Now I have to add immediately that some of the reasons are not related to the book, but by the medium used. Paper. And that's where we, the new generation of indie authors have a HUGE advantage over our predecessors.

Unfortunately, it's not all wine and roses. Marketing takes time, effort and patience. But don't be discouraged. Now that you have your book ready, you should try everything to make it a success.

Welcome to the amazing world of indie publishing!

Who is this book for

This book is for authors that have written an eBook and that are now confronted with the question: How do I sell it? This book is written for people that publish their book on Amazon, although about 80% of the advice can also be applied to other publishing platforms. No special knowledge is required.

All things are explained in easy to understand language. You will find valuable information in this book if you are completely new to the eBook publishing business. Or if you already have published a couple of books, but they're not selling the number of copies that you had hoped or expected.

Who this book is NOT for

If you have already sold 100.000 books, or if you have published already 20 titles, part of that success is probably caused by the fact that you master for at least 80% of what is in this book. Or maybe even more. Or you have outsourced the complete marketing of your books. In that case, and applying the famous 80/20 rule, I don't think you will find any golden ideas here.

But now you're there, keep reading and let me know what you think of my eBook. I would really appreciate your feedback.

Another much broader question you may ask yourself: Should you sell eBooks rather than doing affiliate marketing? Or building a list? Or creating your own Clickbank product? Or creating a video course? This is a whole other topic and clearly out of the scope of this book. But I might write another one on that topic.

A new indie author is born!

Every author starts one day with selling the first copy of his first book. And I can tell you that that is a marvelous moment of joy and happiness. And I'm sure this will be confirmed by a lot of authors.

Here you are, a new indie writer, and you maybe have been writing for weeks, or months, and sometimes years. You have spent a lot of time to put your creation on the world. It's almost like giving birth to a baby (Cannot really confirm that one, being a man).

And now, somewhere in the world, someone has bumped onto your book and said to himself: "Ok, I'll buy that one". Unconsciously eliminating tens if not hundreds of other books.

That's a major achievement.

In case you didn't know: An indie writer is an independent or "self-publishing" writer of eBooks. Not to be confused with a newbie writer, which is an author who is completely new to writing. But even if you have self-published 30 eBooks, you still remain an indie writer or author.

How indie authors are taking over traditional publishing

Did you know that the first patented electronic book or eBook dates from 1949? It was written by Angela Ruiz Robles.

Now this is not a history book so I will fast forward a couple of decennia. And then we arrive in 2007 where sales of eBooks started to grow exponentially thanks to the Kindle reader created by Amazon. Followed later on in 2010 by the iPad from Apple.

Because we are going to talk about electronic publishing of eBooks, it may be a good moment to think about how this whole publishing worked in prehistory, with paper books.

Because than you will start to grasp the enormous opportunity that has been created just recently with this whole self-publishing industry.

Loooong time ago, (let's say pre-2000), when you wrote a book and you wanted to have it published and distributed in bookshops, you had to go over a long and winding road.

The first thing that you had to do, was finding a publisher. I can imagine how these kinds of meetings went:

(This is after having written 20 publishers and finally there is 1 that invites you for an interview)

You get into this smoky office where there is this guy sitting with his big cigar surrounded with piles of books and manuscripts.

Publisher (PB): "Morning. Please sit down".

Author (AU): "Thank you for inviting me to..."

PB: "Yes, you're welcome. Let's see..." (Dives under his desk to pull out a pile of manuscripts)

PB: "I read your book 'The magnificent five'. Not bad".

AU: "Well, actually, my..."

PB: "I might be interested in publishing it. What about your royalties?"

AU: "Ehhh, my book is called 'Murder in the Dark'. It's a thriller".

PB: "Ah, ok. Well, doesn't really matter. Let's get to the point. I'm a pretty busy man. I'll find your manuscript later on. So what about your royalties?"

AU: "Ehhh, what do you propose?"

PB: "25%".

AU: "That sounds fair".

PB: "That's when you've sold 10.000 copies".

AU: "Oh. And my first copies?"

PB: "Well, normally I don't pay any royalties for the first 500 copies. But because you're a nice guy, I lower that to 490. You see, that's how you can distinguish the honest and credible publishers from the crooks".

AU: "And after these first 490?"

PB: "Then it goes up exponentially. 2% for your next 1000 copies, 4% for the next 2000. Etc. You see, your royalties will double already on the next level".

Au: "And how much would this book sell for?"

PB: "Ehhh, let's see. 500 pages, font size 10, plus transport, plus commission for the store owner, plus advertising, plus my small commission of 60%. That would make about $10 retail price. Of which you will get $200..."

AU: "I would get $200 on a $20 sale??"

PB: "That's for your first 1000 copies sold. After the first 490".

AU: "Ehhh, well, I don't know if..."

PB: "Good. I knew that you would take it. This is of course a onetime offer. Please sign here. And of course, printing costs for the first 490 copies are for you. Can you write me a check for 490x $3 equals $1470? We'll do the accounting for you. "

AU: "I guess I have to think this over".

PB: "Ok. No problem. I'm not a difficult guy. My offer remains valid 24 hours, so if you change your mind, come back tomorrow. Sorry, but the next author is waiting".

AU: "It was a real pleasure meeting you. Thank you"

Maybe this is a bit exaggerated. But I hope you get the idea. When you wanted to publish a paper book in the past, you had to find a publisher. And if you found one, they would take an exorbitant part of total sales to cover all the costs of producing the book, distributing the book, getting it into the stores. And... taking it out of the stores.

Because, as you can imagine, a store has only so much space which is not extendable at will. So your book would end up finally in the bookshops.

For two or three weeks....

And then comes the moment of truth where the shop owners are going to do their math. And the verdict is one or the other:

• Yes, good book. Sold enough copies. Send me more.

• No. Doesn't sell enough copies. I'll put another title in its place. Please take away the remaining copies.

And in the second case, that was the end of your book publishing career. Game over. And you end up with your garage full of your own books.

So in the "old game" your book had a period of a couple of weeks to prove itself. If it didn't sell, it would be binned. Ah, and also... it would also cost you a considerable amount of money. You had to travel to publishers, go to signing sessions, come up with some funds for the first copies. Etc.etc.

Now let's see how this all changed by electronic publishing or self-publishing.

Let me describe the bare minimum what would be required to get a book online, in front of millions of potential customers.

- You need a computer. But who hasn't nowadays? You'll probably have one anyway for your emails to your boss, or to follow your Facebook or Twitter followers. So I'm not counting that investment.

- You need a piece of software to write your book. A lot of authors use Microsoft Word, which isn't free. If you cannot afford that you could use OpenOffice. This is a MS Word clone. And it is FREE.

- Now you have to write your book. This is "just" a matter of putting in your time. I don't count the numerous cups of coffee that you will consume during this process.

- When you have your book, you'll need a cover. You can have one made by a professional designer. Rates go from $5 on fiverr.com and can go up to several hundreds of dollars for a real top-notch designer. I'll handle eBook covers further on in this book. But... if you don't have any money available for this task, you can download GIMP.

This is the free equivalent of Photoshop. Does a more than reasonable job to create a cover with a background image, different layers for text etc.

IF you are going this way, make sure that the free image you are going to use has all the rights associated with it, and that you have the appropriate rights to use it on your cover.

- Now your book is ready. Sign up for a FREE account at Amazon.

- Publish your book. This is free.

- Wait a couple of hours till you get the famous message from Amazon: "Your book has been published".

Mission completed! Your book is online in the biggest bookstore in the world and available to be bought by millions of people. Total costs: $0.

Now your book is sitting there on the electronic shelf. It eats up 0, 000000001% of the total disk space at Amazon. But these are nice guys and they give you this storage for free. So even if your book doesn't move for weeks or months, it will just sit there, taking up electronic dust.

(Note that Amazon reserves the right to un-publish any book for almost any reason they like. But hey, it's their shop)

Now what can/may happen with your book? It may sell a couple of books every month. For weeks or months to come. And then suddenly it goes through what is called a "breakout". Suddenly your sales increase from 2 a month, to 2 a day, to 50 a day, to 500 a day!! And finally, you end up on the NY Times bestseller list.

Now you get invited on TV shows, an interview by Ophrah Winfrey and Spielberg will make a movie about your life.

And all this maybe a year after you had published your book. How come?

Well, "something" happened that suddenly increased your sales exponentially. But what? This can be for several reasons. It can be something plain simple as replacing a dull cheapo cover by a real professional cover that catches the eye.

It may be something minor as changing your Title from your current dull 10 word phrase into a 3 word killer Title.

Or it may be something that has nothing to do with your book. Maybe you write a killer blog post which goes viral. It is picked up by a big blogger who publishes it. And people will start looking at your blog to read other stuff you write. And there they bump onto your books.

Or maybe you did some heroic action like saving a child in your neighborhood. The local newspaper published about it, which gets picked up by a national newspaper, etc.etc.

Now of course, this will not happen to every book from every author. Actually it will be rather rare. But the point I was trying to make is: There is no such thing like the dead-clock ticking as soon as you publish your book.

You have time to do anything (legal) you want or like to make it sell better. Improve the content, improve the cover, put it in other categories, publish more books etc.etc.

And that's a HUGE difference compared with traditional publishing.

Note that you can outsource the whole marketing of your book. In that case, your work ends as soon as you have finished writing the book.

But in my opinion that puts you back into the position where "old-game" authors were. You are now again dependent on a publisher. I don't say that that's a bad idea. But first try to market your book yourself, so that you understand what this is all about.

And when you're at your 5th, 8th or 10th book (yes, you will have to write several books, I'll come back to that), you could maybe consider to outsource the whole marketing part. Either to a publisher or to a VA (Virtual Assistant) who will do all the marketing work for you, but you will still be in charge.

But let's not jump to conclusions about what might happen when you have published 10 books.

Can you become rich as an indie author?

This question is very similar to:

- Can you ever win the national lottery?

- Will your next record sell as good as the album Thriller from Michael Jackson?

- Will your book outsell Harry Potter in the next month?

Mathematically speaking, the correct answer to all the above questions is: Yes. There is a theoretical infinite low probability that this might happen.

And if one day that happens to you, and you have sold 10 million books, I hope you will leave me a review on one of my books. :)

But let's get back to reality. A good part of books published by indie authors will never sell ONE copy! Nil, zero, nadda, none. That's the hard reality.

How come? Part of the explanation is that self-publishing is very easy (and I'm talking now about the process) and cheap. This means that a LOT of people are giving it a try. So the competition is huge. Much more than in the old days when the price of the entry ticket was much higher.

If you just write your book and put it up on one of the platforms, your chances of making any money with it are almost zero. That's why marketing your book is so important. And that's what this book is all about.

There are lots of things you can do to market your book. I have collected every strategy and tip that I could find and added my own bag of ideas. But even then, if you apply everything that I cover in this book, it is no guarantee for success.

I cover a lot of points in this book. But if I had to select the two that seem to be the most important and the most effective to increase your sales, then I would take the following two:

1. Make sure that your book is good. Or even better: That it is excellent. This may sound obvious but if you start reading lots

of eBooks you will notice that a lot of so called "authors" didn't grasp this essential point.

Some grab a couple of articles left and right, scotch them together, take a picture of their garden, put that into GIMP to create their cover, and publish their next 20 page bestseller "How to improve your garden in 8 hours".

Others go even a step further. They grab a 15 page PLR book (which is a completely written eBook that you can get even for free on certain sites) and just publish it "as is".

In my opinion, this is a complete waste of time. Come to think of it, it's nice to know that lots of people publish rubbish like that. At least it means that they are not spending their time on writing GOOD books, which makes it (a little bit) easier for those authors that DO put a lot of time and effort in their books.

As in traditional publishing the most effective thing to get your book sold is word-of-mouth from customers. Try to blow them away. Try to create the "WOWW" effect. The ideal would be that if someone has finished reading your book

-They leave you a 5 star review. That would already be great.

-They want to send as soon as possible an email to their friends, saying: "You HAVE to read this book. NOW".

If you can get there, you stand a pretty good chance to become a bestselling author.

2. Publish several books. This is just dictated by mathematical laws. It's like lottery tickets. If you buy one, your chance to win is very low. But if you buy 50, you have increased your chances substantially. And with publishing this goes even further.

If you publish several books, on a certain moment you will create synergy between those books (assuming that they are more or less in the same category). So when you score a modest success with one of them, people may say: "Hmm, let's see what other books this author has written".

How many books do you need to write? Well, how long is a piece of string? I have no real answer to this. Some people would say "More is better". But even that is not so obvious. If all your books have the same flaws (no good content, no value, spelling errors, no clear story, no plot, etc.etc.), then it doesn't matter if you publish 10, 20 or 50 books. 50 x 0 = 0.

Which brings me back to point 1: Make sure, that your book is as best as you can. What does that mean "make sure"? Well, I don't have the magic formula which defines why a book is "good". What I do know is, that there are a couple of obvious things you should ask yourself, to avoid that your book is considered "bad". Here is a short list:

• Study and read similar books in your field and ask yourself the honest question: Is my book better than all of these? Does it bring more value? Does it have a good story (for fiction)?

• Does the cover look good? And the title and subtitle? Now this is of course very subjective. But you could go as far as testing it out with a poll or other voting mechanism. I'll talk about that later in this book

• Is the writing correct? No spelling errors. You can improve this by having your book proofread by a professional.

And more. But when you hit the publish button you should be able to say to yourself: "Ok, I gave it all I had". If you cannot say that honestly to yourself, potential customers will vote with their wallets and their reviews.

Here is a chart that also sets expectations right.

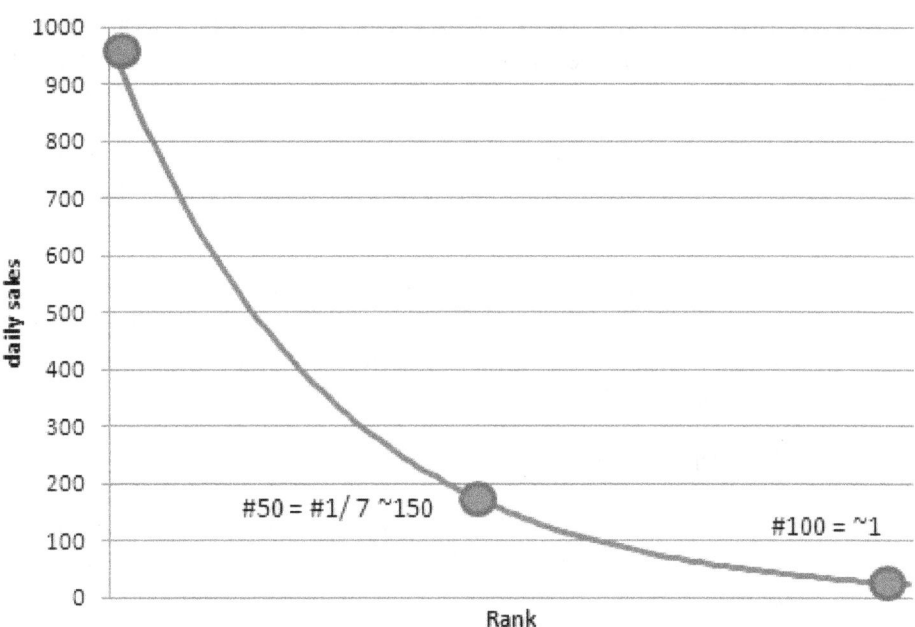

rank versus sales

#50 = #1/ 7 ~150

#100 = ~1

(vertical axis: daily sales, horizontal axis: Rank)

On the vertical axis you see number of sales. On the horizontal axis you see the top X sales rank. Now I haven't set any numbers on the horizontal axis, because this depends a lot on the publishing platform. If your book is on a platform with 100.000 titles, the top X in this graph may represent the top 100. If you are on a platform with 2.000.000 titles this axis may represent the top 500.

But that's not the important point. The important point to take away is: Sales go **exponentially** down with sales rank. Assume that number 1 sells 1000 copies a day (again, this depends on the publishing platform). When you go down half of the top X, this number is already reduced by a factor 7. And when you go to the right of the chart, this number is divided by about 100.

Point to take away: Only a very little percentage of authors are selling hundreds, or sometimes thousands of books a day. I will talk more about daily sales, and specifically for Amazon, further on in this book.

Amazon disclaimer

For my market research for this book, I've gone through a lot of blogs, forums, books, articles and I used my own experience with Amazon.

99.99% of the information from these sources goes something like:"Amazon does this...", "Amazon sales rank works like that...", "Amazon hot releases section shows such..." Etc.

But hardly ever, or maybe I should say never, because I haven't seen any, it is stated:"It has been confirmed by Amazon that...", or "Mr. X at Amazon, Chief marketing eBooks explains that the following works like this..."

Why not? Well, there are several reasons.

1. Like Google's search algorithm where hundreds of parameters are taken into account, Amazon's algorithms for calculating author and sales rankings are ... complex. How complex? They weigh in a lot of factors. Which ones? And how? Weighted averages? Exponential? Logarithmic?

   I don't know. And as far as I can determine, there is not a source where this is published.

2. Put yourself in the shoes of Amazon. You have developed over several YEARS a sophisticated selling machine that uses lots of complicated calculations and algorithms. Would you publish that somewhere? No. Surely not! These will be kept like the crown jewels.

The only reliable source how Amazon works, are the help pages on Amazon itself. And for obvious reasons, on a lot of points, the information on these pages is "approximate" at best. For the very good reason that they don't want to tell you exactly what is going on behind the screens.

Al this means is that what you read on blogs, forums or in books (this one included) is only an interpretation of the author's opinion on how THEY think that Amazon works.

I'm not an Amazon employee, or an Amazon big shot. I don't own Amazon stock. My only relationship with Amazon is that I sell my books there.

Now what can you do if you're confronted with a black box that does "something" , like Google or Amazon, but you don't know exactly what? You feed it with some data at the input side and watch what comes out at the output side.

This is the principal of what is called a perceptron or learning machine. And when lots of people observe the outputs by feeding in different inputs, you can make some reasonable safe interpretations of what is going on inside that black box.

The Truth about Marketing

Before I get into the details about marketing your eBook, I think it is important to set your expectations right. There are basically two ways to sell your books.

1. Selling it yourself. Either on your site or through affiliate marketing.

2. Selling it on a big platform like Amazon, Smashwords, Apple etc.

Or a mixture of these. I will hardly talk about the first option in this book. Why? Because I think that that option only makes sense if you have a site with tens of thousands of visitors a month.

Therefore, I will mainly talk about option 2. And between the different platforms? Well, this is a bit the same when you're getting into search engines. Google has almost 70% of the search engine market. Therefore, if you are going to analyze or optimize your results for a search engine, it is obvious to go for the biggest one first.

Amazon currently has about 50% of the eBook market. Therefore, if you are considering a platform, Amazon is the obvious one to go for first. And there are other reasons that I will cover later on.

Amazon is a huge marketing machine. Started almost 20 years ago. Hundreds of thousands of visitors daily, millions of references, biggest retailer on the internet, very smart marketing and promotion techniques. In short, this is a multi-mega marketing bulldozer.

When you put your product into the Amazon machine, with the right parameters, it gets munched in the Amazon marketing mill and nothing can stop it anymore. And there is little that you can do about it.

So, why should you do any marketing at all?? Well, truth is indeed that your sales results will depend for 60-70% on the Amazon marketing power. This means that anything YOU will do afterwards, will contribute to the remaining 30-40%.

The only thing that you can do yourself is sending traffic to Amazon. You can spend hours, days, weeks and months on all kinds of marketing tricks to do that. But never forget the important 80/20 rule, which I will quote several times throughout this book. 80% of your results will be obtained with 20% of the things you undertake.

This means that if you apply EVERYTHING what I have written in this book your sales WILL increase. But it is very unlikely that they will EXPLODE due to your marketing efforts alone. IF your sales explode it's very likely that your book is very good and that Amazon puts it therefore in front of a maximum number of eyeballs.

Think about how many leads you can send per day to Amazon compared with the hundreds of thousands of customers that get there in any other way. 10? 100? 1000?

That's why I am sometimes amused when I see certain articles, blogs or books where the author claims: "if you bold your titles in your description, that will increase your sales by at least 30%". "If you add a picture to your author profile that will increase your sales with 20%". Etc.etc. If you would apply the 50 tips that are written in such a book, your sales would increase at least with 500% if you add it all up. I call that, marketing of their marketing book.

Sounds great, but unfortunately, that's not the way it works.

Now, there are a couple of exceptions to what I just wrote. If you have a BIG email list of 50.000 subscribers or more, then using that list in your marketing efforts will make a huge difference. But I think that IF you are in that category, I don't have to explain to you what the value of a list is.

For the others: Yes, building a list is an important activity online. But this book is NOT about how to build a list. It's about how to sell books.

The same holds if you have a very prominent presence somewhere else: If you have a Facebook following of 100.000 people or 50.000 followers on twitter, or your own television or radio show, that WILL make a big difference if you deploy these marketing channels.

But I think that the majority of the readers of this book will not fall into any of these categories.

To resume: Never forget that your marketing efforts come ON TOP of the 10.000 horsepower engine of Amazon. That puts in perspective what you can expect from your marketing efforts.

Good, now that we have set expectations right, let's get into the meat of this book and get into all the things you can do to market your book and sell more books!

Where to publish your book?

Although this book mainly discusses publishing on Amazon, there are other platforms on which you could publish your book. The biggest ones are iBookstore from Apple, Barnes & Noble, Sony, Kobo, Baker & Taylor, The Diesel eBook Store.

To get your book published on these platforms the simplest is to submit your book on Smashwords who will then publish your book onto all these platforms.

But you can only do so, if you haven't done an exclusivity agreement with Amazon. The choice is up to you. When you don't give exclusivity to Amazon, and you also publish it on Smashwords you will reach more potential readers. On the other hand, your Amazon sales will be less, because if you don't give exclusivity to Amazon, you cannot use their promotion tools.

This is a personal choice for which you have to make up your mind yourself.

How to market your book?

There are probably hundreds of tricks and strategies you can use to market your book. And I have tried to be as complete as possible in this book. Have I used all these strategies myself? No. Why not?

If I had to apply ALL strategies included in his book on ALL my current (and future) books, I probably would spend 90% of my time on marketing.

This on its turn would mean that I wouldn't have any time left to write new books. And writing is what I like. For me, the marketing is a necessary activity. But it is not my favorite hobby. Nevertheless, I do have to spend some time on it.

And always remember the 80/20 rule. When you apply 100 marketing strategies to your book(s), 20% of these will make 80% of the difference in the final result. So, the message here is: don't get carried away with all this marketing stuff. Yes, it is important. But you don't have to do it ALL. And you can do certain things over time. Remember, your book will not get binned if it hasn't sold a copy for the first couple of months.

Another reason is that I don't agree with all the strategies written in this book. This may sound strange. But there are a certain number of grey hat and black hat strategies that people use. I don't. But to make this book as complete as possible, I felt obliged to at least write something about these tricks. Up to you to decide if you're going to use them or not with all the possible consequences.

I would suggest that you pick a certain number of things out of this book and see how that works and if it has some effect. And in the meantime, write your next book.

If the marketing has some effect, and you have made some sales, put in another trick or improvement. If after all your efforts, and after months of trying, your book is still going nowhere, you have to come to one and only one honest conclusion: Your book doesn't interest readers.

I agree, that's a harsh conclusion. But it's reality. Not every book can sell hundreds of copies a day. Actually, only a small percentage will. But don't get discouraged by that. It might even stimulate you to do even better with your next book. And the next.

Successful eBook publishing is a matter of sticking to it for the long term. Don't expect overnight success in 3 months with 3 books. And if they don't sell, keep trying and improving. The only way in this business to succeed is to be in it for the long haul.

Checklist for your book

Although this book is not about HOW to write a book, it may be useful to include a checklist to verify that your book includes all necessary items before you publish it and before you are going to market it. If you think that your book is already up to publishing standards then you can skip immediately to the next chapter. If not, here is a checklist of things that you have to verify before you even think about publishing.

• Is your book good enough?

This is the one and most important question that you have to ask yourself. I already covered this extensively in the previous chapter.

• Table of Contents.

This should be a linked list, without page numbers.

Note that all front matter is part of what will be shown in the preview or "look inside" feature on Amazon. This means that if you make all the front matter too long (2 pages copyright, 5 pages TOC etc.) your readers may only get 1 or 2 pages of the actual content of your book. The 'look inside' feature will show approximately 10% of the top of your book.

So, if you write a short book with lots of headings, and you include these all in your TOC, the TOC will be relatively long compared to the total book size. And chances are, that the 'look inside' feature will only show your front matter. Therefore, you should always check, as soon as your book is published, what shows up in the 'look inside' feature.

That's also one of the reasons, why I move all the items that are not really compulsory for the front matter to the back matter. For example, a disclaimer.

Some authors go as far, as putting the table of contents (TOC) to the end of their book. And one could argue that the TOC is just a list of links anyway, so it doesn't really matter where it is located. Well, I won't discuss this in length. For me, a TOC has to be at the beginning of the book. And that's where I put mine.

It is NOT compulsory to include ALL your headings of level 1, 2, 3 etc. in your TOC. If you write your book with Word (or OpenOffice) and you decide to use the automatic TOC generation you can specify up to which level you want to include your (sub-) headings.

Some platforms, like Smashwords, ask you to include a manually generated TOC. This, to be able to generate a so called NCX file. I will not go into detail here about how to format your book. If you want to know all the details about HOW to format your Word document so that it comes out professionally on all devices (PCs, Kindles, iPad), please read my book "The Ultimate Kindle Formatting Guide".

• Is your Front matter complete?

Front matter is all the parts that appear before the real start of your book. Compulsory items are: Title (& Subtitle if appropriate), Copyright, Table of Contents.

Optional items are: Blurbs, Disclaimer

Blurbs: certain writers include, before anything else, testimonials of readers of their book. This ensures that when potential buyers use the preview or "look inside" feature, they see immediately what other people have said about this book (according to the author). For example:

"This is a great book to learn all ins and outs of marketing eBooks. I highly recommend this book"

Mr. Unknown

Personally, I have never used these, so I don't know if this is very effective or not. It goes without saying that these testimonials have to be REAL testimonials.

Title Page: The Title Page is the page that contains only: The Title, Subtitle and name of the author(s). Centered. Preferably in a larger font size. Also put the copyright on the title page and include your website. This will ensure that if people use the 'Look inside' feature, they will immediately see the name of your website.

Copyright: To protect your book, you have to include a copyright chapter. You can find numerous examples all over the internet. What is important is, that you make it clear that nothing may be copied, rewritten, photocopied etc. without written permission of the author.

• Length of your book

Concerning the length of your book (nr of words): All studies show that, the longer your book is, the more it will sell. Of course, these studies are conducted over thousands, if not hundreds of thousands of books. And the exception confirms the rule.

Moreover, there is a big difference between fiction and non-fiction. If you write a fiction book the "minimum" word count seems to be 80.000 words. (Yes, that's a lot). But real bestsellers go up to 100.000 or 150.000 words or more!! Just so that you know that when you write your new thriller of 30.000 words and it doesn't sell, this might give you a clue.

On the opposite side, if you write non-fiction, like How-to guides, advice, teaching books etc. more is not always better. Sure, a 300 page "Bible" book about "How to Photoshop" will probably sell better than a quick 30-page copy on how to open a PSD file and how to save a JPG. But if you write a 300-page book about "How to grow plants on your balcony", I'm not sure that you will sell more than a 50-page book that gets right to the point.

Non-fiction books often treat a specific problem for their audience. The person that bought your book has THAT specific problem, and if you can write that down in 50 pages then they will be more inclined to buy it then a 500-page reference book. They have a problem and they want to have it solved NOW. The sooner the better.

Having said all this, I think the bottom line is: Your reader wants to get value for his money. A novel reader wants to have a complete story. With characters, situations, twists, surprises etc. So, a 10.000-word book will just not cut it.

For a non-fiction self-help book like "How to stop smoking", IF you could write a 10.000-word book on that one, with really GREAT value, it might become a bestseller. But you will experience yourself when you write several books, that explaining something in detail and adding enough value, will take a lot more than 10.000 words.

• The length of your title (and subtitle)

This one is the opposite of the length of your book. Shorter is better. A Title "Lose 10 pounds a week" will hook more readers than "The Best Vegetable Diet That Will Make You Lose 10 Pounds in a Week".

(I agree, both are not brilliant).

But this is one of the reasons that copy writers are paid a fortune for good titles. Because the contradiction in terminus is: How to say more with less. And that's not easy.

• Links in your book

Don't include affiliate links. In general, this is not accepted by the different distributers (Apple, Amazon etc.). Having said that, my experience is that if you publish a book on Amazon and you include 1 or 2 affiliate links to other products on Amazon, that will pass. I said 1 or 2. Not a hundred.

Link to your own website: You should include a link to your own website, so that readers may find out more about you or subscribe to your email list. A good location to do that is in your "About the Author" chapter or your "Contact" chapter. Another good location is, to put it on the Title Page in your book, right under the author's name.

Links to your blog: Sometimes you may be writing on something that you have covered already extensively in a blog post. Now you can do two things: Either copy the article in your book, or just create a link to your blog post.

The first solution has the advantage that the reader doesn't have to be connected to the internet to see what you're talking about. On the other hand, if you include 20 articles that have been published already on your blog, and your readers are also following your blog, they may not appreciate this. To be used moderately.

Progress tracking links: Some authors include in their books so called progress tracking links to track exactly how far readers got through their book. I don't use these myself, but this is the idea behind it:

You include after every chapter/section a different bitly link (see bitly.com to learn how to do this). Sure, it has to make some sense in the context of your book. Something like "This is end of chapter 1, please click here" will not work :(. But maybe "If you want to have more detail about what was described in this chapter, click here". (Which should bring the reader really to an interesting page with even more information related to chapter one).

If you do this for every chapter in your book, AND you sell a significant number of books (let's say at least 100 a month), then after a couple of months when you have a significant amount of data, you might analyze all this data to get some idea how far people got through your book. Personally, I think this strategy falls into the wrong side of the 80/20 rule. But at least you're aware of it.

Verify your links: Before publishing do verify all the links and bookmarks in your book. In Word: click on "Insert Link" and "Insert bookmark" to verify that there are no unknown links and bookmarks left in your book.

• Should you use a pen name?

Before you publish your book, you'd better decide if you publish it under your real name or under a pen name. There are several reasons why you would decide to take a pen name.

1. You want to completely separate your online life from your life in the real world. In this case you would make up a completely invented person. Name, photo, age etc.

2. You have an unpronounceable name like "Geronimo Abrawokimitz". In this case it may be interesting to just use a pen name for your first/last name, but for the rest use your real Personal information (photo, country etc.). There are lots of sites on internet to help you with finding a pen name. Just type into Google "pen name generator".

3. You have written already several books in one category, for example fitness, and now you want to publish books in a completely different category, like children's books or dating. If you would use the same author name for all these books, this may confuse potential customers.

When they fall onto your author profile and they see the titles "How to get fit in 20 days", "Feeling fitter every day" and "Peter Pan and the green frog", they may be wondering what your expertise is. Therefore, in such a case, it is better to write the other category under a pen name.

Notice that on Amazon you can use 3 pen names, each with their own author profile, picture etc. However, on your Author Central page, you can aggregate these 3 identities into 1, so that all reporting for the different pen names will be done from 1 dashboard.

Just a last word about pen names. Some people use pen names because they assume that doing so, no one will find out who the real author is behind a title. Well, if you still think that anything can pass unnoticed on internet, it is time to wake up.

The fact that maybe people haven't checked you (or your pen name) out, is because they don't want to know more about you.

But the moment you hit a bestseller list somewhere, certain people WILL go and find out who is behind the title.

- Verify the back matter

Back matter is all the things that you add to the end of your book, but which are not directly related to the content of your book.

Certain authors add some kind of separation between the front matter and the real start of the book, and between the end of the book and the back matter.

Something like "###" or "~~~" or "~~~===~~~". Up to you to decide if you want to use these.

What should/could you include in the back matter?

Ask for a review: There is nothing wrong with asking your readers for an honest review. Notice that I said "an honest review". Not an "honest positive review" or "a positive review". You have to accept that sooner or later you will get a more or less negative review. That's part of the game. If you get one, don't worry too much about it. Continue with your next book, instead of going into an endless discussion with Amazon or the customer if the review is justified or not.

About the Author: You can include a short section on "About the author", in which you explain a bit who you are, what you do, why you write books etc. You could even include a picture of yourself. The whole purpose is to connect with your readers.

Contact: You can include a "Contact" section, in which you include all your contact details like: Facebook fan page, twitter account, Google+ account, RSS feed, website and email address.

Other books from the author: If you have several books, the ideal place to promote your other books is the back matter. If you have only 1 or 2 other books, you can include the covers and an excerpt of these books with a link to these books on Amazon. If you have 4-5 books or more, only include excerpts of the books that are directly related to the current book.

Again, don't overdo it. If you have 15 other books, don't include 3 pages of excerpts to these other books. Instead, you could redirect people directly to your author page or setup a special domain or page on your website where you have a listing of all your books.

Do use Amazon affiliate links to your books instead of direct links! I'll describe this extensively in the chapter "Tracking Sales and other data".

Tip for back matter: Your back matter will be substantially the same for all your books. If you have planned to write 5, 10 or 20 books then you can of course copy and paste all the back matter from one book to the other. But imagine that you now want to change something in this back matter after having published book 10, because you have figured out that something works better, or you got a good tip from someone.

You now have to open all your previous books and apply the changes one by one on all your book files. A smarter way to do this is to put your back matter in a separate file, and include it only when you are going to produce your book for Amazon.

Freebie: If you have a freebie on your site, include it here. Some readers may be interested in your free book/report/software. And that will result in a new subscriber to your list. I will not go into lengthy detail here about the importance of your email list, because that is not the subject of this book. But just let me make ONE remark: If the sale (or the free give-away during a promotion) of your book results in a subscription to your list, you have achieved a VERY valuable result.

Disclaimer: I always include a disclaimer. The content depends on the type of book I am writing. If you write a book that includes links to external pages, always include a disclaimer that you cannot guarantee the proper functioning of these links because they are out of your control.

When you write a book that talks about gaining something (money, audience, visitors, views, stop smoking), always include a disclaimer that the things you discuss are not a proof of sure success.

• Create a great cover.

On this subject alone, I could write a bible. And there are hundreds, if not thousands of articles and books about cover design, how to find good titles, color schemes etc. That's why creating a good cover is an art and not a science. As is getting a good title. But you don't have to spend thousands of dollars on these. If you're not proficient with graphics software, outsource the design.

Try to come up with the title and subtitle yourself. I wouldn't outsource that to someone else. Unless I had the budget to hire a professional who has a track record of hundreds of good book titles.

But don't get hang up on this one either. Yes, spend some time on your cover. But if it isn't good (and there are ways to find out), you can always change it later on.

Now creating a good cover sounds obvious, but do the following test yourself. Go onto Amazon into the Kindle eBook section and just click on any category. You will now see 10-15 covers. Just browse the covers that come up. Don't read in detail the title and subtitles. Just scan quickly the images. Take a piece of paper and just make a cross when a cover immediately catches your eye.

Do this for 100 or 200 titles. Will take you 10 minutes. And you will be amazed how few crosses you have on your paper. If you get to 10, that's a lot. Conclusion: The far majority of the covers don't have that little touch which makes it stand out between all the others. Now go back and take a closer look at the covers that you ticked off. What made it that they grabbed your eye?

They probably have one or more of the following:

1. Catchy bright colors. It's amazing how many grey shade dull covers there are.

2. A title that you can read. All studies that have been done on the subject of titles come to the same conclusion: Short is better. And this counts especially for eBooks where your cover is displayed on a listing page as a 120x160 pixel image (approximately). Before deciding on your cover, always resize it to that size and see if at least your title is still readable

3. A subtitle that is also readable on that size. This is a real challenge for the designers, because normally the subtitle is smaller than the title and often longer. But don't take a 20-word subtitle.

4. Use words that are known to "hook" a potential reader. New, free, you, secret etc.

5. Make a list of 10-15 titles. And 10-15 subtitles. Put it away. The fact that you have written them down makes that they are recorded somewhere in your brain. Your unconscious will keep working on these. Even while you're asleep. After a couple of days, pull out the list and scrap of 3 or 4 of each. Repeat till you have 3 or 2 left for each.

Now take your cover and make a mockup of your cover. You now end up with 2 or 3 covers. Run these as a CPC campaign on Facebook. This is very easy to do. See my chapter on Facebook promotion. Let it run for 2-3 days. This will cost you $5-$10 and will give you thousands of views, but more importantly, you will see which cover people will click on the most. Simple, fast and reliable.

6. In the same way, and if you don't want to bother with Facebook, do a brainstorm session with 4 or 5 people. Or post your 2 or 3 possible titles on writer forums like Goodreads, the Amazon community or other forums that are specifically related to the subject/topic of your book.

7. And why not read some books on how to find good covers and titles?

Titles & Covers That Sell - How to Create a Killer Title and Captivating Cover to Maximize Your Book Sales

The Complete Book Cover Creation Guide: What makes a good cover and how to create your own for FREE. Update 2022

Remember, your cover doesn't have to be the best one in the world. It just has to be a bit better than the competition. So, if only 1 on 10-15 covers stand out, it shouldn't be too difficult to make one that stands out also, doesn't it?

Important: When you outsource the creation of your cover, ask from the designer proof that the image(s), clipart or whatever he used has the appropriate copyrights. If the designer uses an image or picture from another site or he hasn't paid the royalties, YOU are responsible in case someone is going after you.

Tip: Always make a backup cover. Even something very simple. Just in case. It might happen that for whatever reason your cover is going to create a problem. Someone claims rights on the image or clipart, some people are offended by picture XYZ or whatever. In such a case, where you have to react FAST, you can use then your backup cover.

Other Do's and Don'ts

Here are a couple of other things to keep in mind, before we get to the prelaunch phase.

- **Don't borrow.** I felt obliged to include this point in my book, after having read some horror stories on the internet about people borrowing money to try, by all means, to push their book up in the charts.

Typically, this may go something like this. They write and publish their book almost for free. Not because they don't want to spend some money on it, but because they just don't have any spare money to spend.

The book doesn't fly. Hmmm, must be my cover. So, they get that redone by a professional designer. Who gets paid with money that was borrowed from a friend, family or whoever. Hey, you're soon going to be a top writer, so you'll have your money back within no time.

Book still doesn't fly. Or worse, it sells some copies. Now the author really gets hooked and smells "the big fortune". How to boost this quickly? Let's try some Facebook or other PPC advertising. $20 here, $30 there etc.

Great! Sold another 2 copies. From 1 to 4 is indeed a HUGE increase percentage wise. Ok. Let's take out some real cash and spend $300 on a course that will teach me how to sell eBooks.

Etc. The obvious outcome from all of this is that you just keep digging a big (financial) hole and at the end you even might lose a friend.

So, sound advice: Spend whatever money you wish on boosting your sales. As long as it is your money and it is money you can afford to lose. This is not specific to just selling books, but valid for any business adventure.

- **Don't buy expensive courses**. Not that they aren't worth the money. Actually, there are some good ones out there. But most of the information you need is available online in forums, blogs. And for $20 you can buy a couple of good books! :)

- **Don't give up your job!** This sounds like a no-brainer but some people consider this option after having published 2 books and sold 50 copies. Yes, writing takes a lot of time. And if you have a job and you can only write evenings and weekends it will even take longer. But just calculate quickly how many books you have to sell before you generate the same income of $1500 that you get for your lousy job.

To get $1500 net in your pocket, and if you set this up as a genuine business where you now have to pay yourself for all the expenses and you don't have a company car or free flyer miles anymore you should make something around the $3000 mark. Of course, this depends a lot on the country you're living in. $100 in India is not the same as $100 in the US.

If you make $2 on a book, you need to sell 1500 copies. A month. And not just one month but every month.

Again, this is NOT impossible. But wait till you get around those figures before you jump ship.

- **Do setup a website**. This is not compulsory, but it will help a lot in all your marketing efforts. You don't have to do this immediately before you publish your first book. But on the other hand, creating a basic website with Wordpress is within the reach of almost anybody. But there are lots of authors out there who don't have a website. I don't know if they are successful or not.

To conclude this chapter: There are three things of value considering your book:

• A sale

• A positive review

• A subscription to your list.

If you sell your book AND the reader gives you a 5-star review AND he subscribes to your list, you have scored a homerun!!

The prelaunch

So, you have your book ready. You have gone through the previous checklist and you're ready to publish your book. Wait!

In the prelaunch phase, you should do a certain number of things, so that everything is ready at launch day to ensure that your marketing efforts have the maximum impact.

You should start with these activities at least 2 weeks in advance of Launch Day. Note that launch day is the day that your promotion campaign really starts. This is different from the publishing day. Why? Because to prepare your promotion you need the ASIN of your book.

The ASIN number is a unique book identification number that you get from Amazon when you publish your book. Therefore, the normal sequence is: Publish your book and schedule your promotion 1 or 2 weeks later on.

If you're really in a hurry you can do this a bit different to shorten this a bit. Suppose that your cover isn't ready yet, but you know that it will be there in a couple of days. What you could do is: publish your book with a replacement cover, get the ASIN , un-publish your book and start the promotion activities.

When you publish your book a week later with the real cover you will get the same ASIN. But notice that the Amazon T&C's specify that you can only publish books that are complete.

So put that in your plan if you haven't written or finished your book yet.

Ehhh, yes, I do suggest that you make a **plan** when you start writing your book.

Here is a sample plan I use:

Task Name	Duration	Start	Finish		July				August			September		
					E	B	M	E	B	M	E	B	M	E
− Book nr X	25 days?	Tue 01/07/14	Sun 27/07/14											
Research	4 days	Tue 01/07/14	Fri 04/07/14											
Outline	1 day?	Sat 05/07/14	Sat 05/07/14											
Title	0.5 days?	Tue 22/07/14	Wed 23/07/14											
Order cover	3 days	Wed 23/07/14	Sat 26/07/14											
Write	15 days	Sun 06/07/14	Tue 22/07/14											
Proofread	4 days	Tue 22/07/14	Sat 26/07/14											
Prepare promotion KDF	1 day?	Mon 14/07/14	Tue 15/07/14											
Publish	1 day?	Sat 26/07/14	Sun 27/07/14											
− Promotion	50 days	Sun 03/08/14	Thu 25/09/14											
KDP promotion 3 days	3 days	Sun 03/08/14	Wed 06/08/14											
KDP promotion 2 days	2 days	Tue 23/09/14	Thu 25/09/14											

Of course, a lot depends on how long you plan for the writing. If you have planned to write a 300.000-word novel, that will occupy you for a couple of months (at least), and you will not be on a week close to start with your prelaunch activities.

However, if you're a serial writer who cranks out every 3-4 weeks a book, then an overall planning is really necessary, because after 3 or 4 books, you won't remember what you have done or not for each book.

If you have already finished your book (but not published it yet), well, then you have no choice. Then you have to go first through these prelaunch activities if you want your marketing campaign to have some success.

Notice that you don't HAVE to do all of the following activities. The more you do, the more it will help. But there are certain activities that have more impact than others

In this chapter I will cover things like:

• Preparing your Keywords

• Analyzing the competition

• Amazon categories

• Preparing a submission file

• Pricing

• Site submissions

• KDP select and Countdown deals

Keywords

How do buyers find your book when it is published? Sure, if you have a mailing list of 50.000 subscribers that helps. But most of the readers of this book will not have such a list.

You're also going to announce it through all kinds of other media (free websites, YouTube, etc.). And that helps. I will handle all that further on in this book.

But the majority of people will get to your book by landing on Amazon. Then, they fall into the hands of an enormous marketing giant, who excels into marketing all the stuff that they have for sale. Not that you don't have to do anything anymore and sit back. But having the marketing bulldozer of Amazon working for you will really make the difference.

So back to the initial question: How do buyers find your book? Smashwords has published an interesting study on their blog which you can find here

I won't go into all the details but let me resume the main results of this marketing study and what works best to sell your book(s):

1. Word-of mouth. This accounts for about 30%. That's everything which includes: recommendations from friends, online

41

communities and other people that a potential buyer will trust. Problem for you as a starting writer is: How do you get word-of-mouth if you have no visibility yet? The same holds for the number two in this list...

2. **Author brand.** 18% of buyers go and look for their favorite authors. It is clear that you don't become a recognized author overnight. This takes a lot of time and effort and probably 6 months to a year to get anywhere on the scale of 'favorite authors' (if ever).

3. **Random browsing.** This overlaps for a good part with the previous 2 points and therefore can climb up to about 80%! That's anything from "I just go onto the book store and I browse the categories", "I just browse free books sites", "I look for books to review" etc.

In short, those buyers didn't have a specific idea what they were going to buy when they went online. "It just happened".

And this is a category where even the starting author can benefit from, because it has not so much to do with your sales or your history as an author.

Random browsing can be subdivided in:

• Someone might just browse through the categories. For example, someone who is looking for 'classic cars' would have to browse through:

Kindle eBooks -> Nonfiction -> Professional & Technical -> Automotive -> Classic Cars.

And every time that he clicks on one of these categories, a number of book covers will be displayed on his screen on the right. Which may catch his eye... So do the counting with me: Above I have mentioned 5 categories and their subcategories. On every click he will see something like 10 titles. That's 50 titles in total.

And if he doesn't browse immediately to the right sub category, he will first go through a couple of other categories and sub categories before he gets into the right one. So, you can add easily another 50 titles. That's 100 titles. And yours may be one of them...

I'll go much more extensively into categories and subcategories further on in this book.

- Someone types in a couple of words because he is looking for a topic but without having a specific title or author in mind. Something like 'classic cars' or 'horror stories. And this is where your title/subtitle AND your keywords come into play.

The last point brings us to the importance of keywords. Amongst all the things that you have (or may) fill out when you submit your book, one of the most important fields is the one with your keywords.

You may fill in maximum 7 keywords for your book. Here are some things you should consider when selecting your 7 keywords:

- Use all 7 of them. The more you use, the bigger the chance that your book will show up in a specific query.

- A keyword can actually consist of several words. So, it doesn't have to be a list of just 7 words, separated by a comma.

- Use keywords that describe as much as possible what your book is about. Make a list of at least 20 keywords when you start writing your book. From time to time, throw a glimpse on it and remove some. Until you have the 7 best left.

- Use the predictive search feature from Amazon. This works exactly the same way as in Google. I have written a 148-page book "Find GOLDEN Keywords with FREE Software. Dig up GOLDEN Nuggets with Google Keyword Planner". You can find it here. This explains you in detail how to find good keywords for your articles, website and other writings. So why not use it for your book?

But let me explain with a short example how this works and how you can take advantage of this predictive search. Suppose I'm now an author of a book about classic cars. How and where to find them, how to restore them, how to maintain them etc. And I have come up with the keywords:

- Classic car repair

- Old-timers

- Car repair

Now I'm going to put those words to the test with Amazon's predictive search. In the search bar on the top, I type in the word classic (don't hit ENTER). Now I see:

ore ▾	classic|
I Search	**classics**
g *Find*	**classics** on kindle free
	free **classics**
	classic books
	classic literature
	classic novels
	free **classic** kindle books
	classical music
	delphi **classics**
	classical guitar

Hmm, nothing with cars. I now add a space after the word classic. I get:

ed Searcl   **classic** books

ng *Find*   **classic** literature

classic novels

free **classic** kindle books

free **classic** books

classic science fiction

classic mysteries

free **classic** literature kindle books

classic fiction

classic goosebumps

Again. No cars :(Notice that the words that are shown by Amazon are actual words that have been typed in by real visitors. (You see the first 10 results). Apparently, there are not a lot (if any) visitors searching for "classic car repair".

I repeat the same exercise for the second keyword "old-timers" (or oldtimers" or "old timers"). Again, nothing pops up.

The third keyword "car repair".

car   ← space after car

car charger in Kindle Store

car charger in All Departments

car charger in Electronics

car charger in Automotive

car charger in Cell Phones & Accessories

car and driver

car sales

car charger for kindle fire

car repair

car stereo

car seat covers

car racing

car detailing

car games

Good. Here we have something. And indeed 'car repair' is typed in frequently by visitors. So, I select the keyword 'car repair' from the list. I now look at the left which categories come up.

1-48 of 282 results for **Kindle Store** : "car repair"

Show results for

‹ Any Category

Kindle Store

  Automotive Repair (207)

  Automotive (234)

  Trucks & Vans (4)

  Kindle eBooks (280)

 - See Less

LOOK

Auto Re

DUMM

Auto Repair

And I see in which categories this keyword is used. This is valuable information. I keep my keyword 'car repair' and I make a note of the categories (just right click and bookmark them to a bookmark list). I also skip quickly through the titles. The first 15 titles are books about general maintenance on any car. Nothing specific to classic cars.

On N° 16 I see the first book that is a bit on the same topic as my book:

Low-Cost Car Restoration Vol. 2: Brilliant Bodies and Marvellous Mechanicals by Steve

I click on it to see how it ranks:

Amazon Best Sellers Rank: #359,253 Paid in Kindle Store (See Top 100 Paid in Kindle Store)
#29 in Kindle Store > Kindle eBooks > Nonfiction > Professional & Technical > Automotive > Classic Cars
#67 in Kindle Store > Kindle eBooks > Nonfiction > Professional & Technical > Automotive > Repair

Rank 350.000+. Published June 2013. 2 reviews. All this indicates that this is not really a high selling book. Actually, it may have sold only a few copies. Conclusion: my 'car repair' keyword is maybe not as good as I thought. Normal, because I haven't used classic in my query.

I hope the process is clear. Find keywords that people are indeed searching for.

What's the difference if I would have typed in straight 'car repair' followed by ENTER? I would have seen the same results, but I wouldn't have known that this is a keyword that visitors are actually searching for.

- You can do the same thing with your keywords in Google. Use the predictive search capability of Google to see what people are actually looking for. For more details about Google keywords, see my full book on the subject. This will also explain how to do this with Google Keyword Planner but that's out of the scope of this book.

- Use one of the keywords that Amazon suggests to be listed in a specific category. Huh? What's that? Yes, Amazon publishes a list of keywords for all major categories and subcategories specifying that if you want your book to appear in category XYZ, you should include the keyword(s) ABC in your submission form.

Very nice of them, isn't it? And it cannot get any easier than that. Here is the full listing from Amazon.

Categories with Keyword Requirements

Note that this listing is mainly useful for fiction books.

- Go to the category where you want to list your book. If you don't know that yet, read the chapter on categories first. Now look through the competing books on the same subject. Take one and scroll down to the bottom of the page. Now you see the categories where this book is attached to. Either through its title OR its keywords.

Make a note of these categories. Now you can use one of these categories as a category for your own book OR you can use certain terms as a keyword. For example: I have selected two categories for my book. Now I see a competing book that is listed in the category

Business & Money > Skills > Business Writing

which is not one of the categories that I have selected for my book. Now I could decide to use 'Business Writing' as a keyword.

Check it out with the Amazon predictive search if it is a good keyword.

When you have your keywords, check with the free Google planner tool the search volume on Google.

Competition

Another good thing to do is to study the competition. How do you find books that will be competing with yours?

- By typing in the title that you have in mind for your book. If there are similar titles, or similar books that don't have the same words in their title they might have keywords attached to it that DO appear in **your** title. I go back to my previous example. Suppose that I had in mind a title like "Classic car repairs".

When I type that into the search bar on Amazon, I get:

Modifying Cars From The 50's To 80's Of The 20th Century 2nd Edition by Nik Handford (Jun 1, 2012) - Kindle eBook

$3.63 Kindle Purchase

Auto-delivered wirelessly

⭐⭐⭐☆☆ ☑ (1)

The Cobra Inspired Sports Car Assembly Manual Series Book 1 - Building With or Without a Donor Vehicle by Gary Brizendine (Nov 25, 2012) - Kindle eBook

$4.40 Kindle Purchase

Auto-delivered wirelessly

⭐⭐⭐☆☆ ☑ (1)

(Just picking 2 results out of the result). Notice something? None of these books use "classic" or "repair" in their title. So why do they pop up? They both have indeed "car(s)" in their title. But it is much more likely that they popup because these books are in the right category OR that they have attached to them the keywords "car repair" or "classic car".

The first book in this example is on rank 1 million+ , so for that one we don't see its categories under the product details. (More on that later).

ASIN: B0088CPEDA

Text-to-Speech: Enabled ⌄

X-Ray: Not Enabled ⌄

Lending: Not Enabled

Amazon Best Sellers Rank: #1,464,888 Paid in Kindle Store

For the 2nd one, I see the categories:

Amazon Best Sellers Rank: #239,370 Paid in Kindle Store (See Top 100 Paid in Kindle Store)
    #17 in Kindle Store > Kindle eBooks > Nonfiction > Professional & Technical > Automotive > **Classic Cars**
    #38 in Kindle Store > Kindle eBooks > Nonfiction > Professional & Technical > Automotive > **Repair**

This might be the reason that this one pops up. Because there is a "Classic Car" and a "repair" category. I also notice that, considering the sellers rank, reviews (1) and publishing date (November 2012), this is probably not a very high selling item.

But now, scroll down to the bottom of the page until you get to "Look for similar items by category". Here you will see a couple of categories.

Look for Similar Items by Category

    Books > Engineering & Transportation > Automotive > Classic Cars

    Books > Engineering & Transportation > Automotive > Repair & Maintenance

    Kindle Store > Kindle eBooks > Professional & Technical > Automotive > Classic Car

    Kindle Store > Kindle eBooks > Professional & Technical > Automotive > Repair

What does this mean? That the keyword you just typed ("classic car repairs") is attached to these categories!

How can you put this to your advantage? Unfortunately, Amazon will not show you the keywords that are attached to a book. The only way to find out is by trial and error and deduction. Let's illustrate with an example how to exploit this:

When I wrote this chapter, I took the above example of classic cars just off-the cuff. And after clicking through all of the categories and books in that category, I came to the conclusion that the above-mentioned title (Low-cost restoration) was the highest bestseller on that subject. So, IF I had the idea to write a book on that, and IF I had done this research upfront, I would have known that it's NEVER going to sell more than a couple of copies a month.

So, to illustrate my above reasoning a bit further in detail, I took up a much bigger challenge. A fiction book. Coming up with good keywords for non-fiction is relatively easy, because you're talking about a very specific topic.

For fiction books this is **much** more complicated. So, for the next example, I put myself in the shoes of an author who has written a 300-page novel. And imagine I have written something similar to "Dracula". A guy who sleeps in a coffin and wakes up in the evenings to find ladies where he can tap some blood out of their throat. I hope you get the idea.

Now some of my keywords might be: horror, blood, Dracula. But I have to verify these and come up with some more. I go through the steps described before.

By this research, I learn that books on the similar topic are published in the categories.

Books > Comics & Graphic Novels > Graphic Novels > Horror

Books > Literature & Fiction > Genre Fiction > Horror

Books > Literature & Fiction > Genre Fiction > Horror > Occult

Books > Literature & Fiction > Contemporary

Books > Literature & Fiction > Classics

Books > Literature & Fiction > Literary

Books > Mystery, Thriller & Suspense > Thrillers > Supernatural

Books > Mystery, Thriller & Suspense > Thrillers > Suspense

Kindle Store > Kindle eBooks > Comics & Graphic Novels

Kindle Store > Kindle eBooks > Literature & Fiction > Horror > United States

Kindle Store > Kindle eBooks > Literature & Fiction > Classics

Kindle Store > Kindle eBooks > Literature & Fiction > Contemporary Fiction

Kindle Store > Kindle eBooks > Literature & Fiction > Horror > Classics

Kindle Store > Kindle eBooks > Literature & Fiction > Horror

Kindle Store > Kindle eBooks > Literature & Fiction > Horror > Occult

Kindle Store > Kindle eBooks > Literature & Fiction > Horror > Short Stories

Kindle Store > Kindle eBooks > Literature & Fiction > Literary Fiction

Kindle Store > Kindle eBooks > Literature & Fiction > Mythology & Folk Tales

Kindle Store > Kindle eBooks > Literature & Fiction > Short Stories

Kindle Store > Kindle eBooks > Mystery, Thriller & Suspense > Suspense > Horror

Kindle Store > Kindle eBooks > Mystery, Thriller & Suspense > Suspense > Occult

Kindle Store > Kindle eBooks > Mystery, Thriller & Suspense > Thrillers

Kindle Store > Kindle eBooks > Religion & Spirituality > Occult > Ghosts & Haunted Houses

Kindle Store > Kindle eBooks > Science Fiction & Fantasy > Fantasy > Fairy Tales

By using the Amazon predictive search feature, the only keywords that survive are "horror" and "Dracula". In this list I can take out all categories that start with "Books". I'll explain later why.

By doing this research I stumble also on the word "vampire". I'll go again through the same sequence and find the categories:

Kindle Store > Kindle eBooks > Romance > Paranormal > Demons & Devils

Kindle Store > Kindle eBooks > Science Fiction & Fantasy > Fantasy > Anthologies & Short Stories

Kindle Store > Kindle eBooks > Romance > Paranormal > Vampires

So my complete list of categories now is:

Kindle Store > Kindle eBooks > Comics & Graphic Novels

Kindle Store > Kindle eBooks > Literature & Fiction > Horror > United States

Kindle Store > Kindle eBooks > Literature & Fiction > Classics

Kindle Store > Kindle eBooks > Literature & Fiction > Contemporary Fiction

Kindle Store > Kindle eBooks > Literature & Fiction > Horror > Classics

Kindle Store > Kindle eBooks > Literature & Fiction > Horror

Kindle Store > Kindle eBooks > Literature & Fiction > Horror > Occult

Kindle Store > Kindle eBooks > Literature & Fiction > Horror > Short Stories

Kindle Store > Kindle eBooks > Literature & Fiction > Literary Fiction

Kindle Store > Kindle eBooks > Literature & Fiction > Mythology & Folk Tales

Kindle Store > Kindle eBooks > Literature & Fiction > Short Stories

Kindle Store > Kindle eBooks > Mystery, Thriller & Suspense > Suspense > Horror

Kindle Store > Kindle eBooks > Mystery, Thriller & Suspense > Suspense > Occult

Kindle Store > Kindle eBooks > Mystery, Thriller & Suspense > Thrillers

Kindle Store > Kindle eBooks > Religion & Spirituality > Occult > Ghosts & Haunted Houses

Kindle Store > Kindle eBooks > Romance > Paranormal > Demons & Devils

Kindle Store > Kindle eBooks > Romance > Paranormal > Vampires

Kindle Store > Kindle eBooks > Science Fiction & Fantasy > Fantasy > Fairy Tales

Kindle Store > Kindle eBooks > Science Fiction & Fantasy > Fantasy > Anthologies & Short Stories

Out of this list, I can skip

Kindle Store > Kindle eBooks > Literature & Fiction > Horror

Because it is not a low-level subcategory. With that I mean: There are other categories underneath it. I also skip the first one "comics" and the 2nd one which is specific US. Because my book is 300 pages, I skip also "Short stories". I also take out "Thrillers" and "fairy tale" (This is not a story that I would read to my kids).

For simpler reading I take out the "Kindle Store>Kindle eBooks" in front of each. Now we have, in table form:

	Name Box A	B	C
1	**Main category**	**L1 sub**	**L2 sub**
2	Literature & Fiction	Classics	
3		Contemporary Fiction	
4		Horror	
5			Classics
6			Occult
7		Literary Fiction	
8		Mythology & Folk Tales	
9	Mystery, Thriller & Suspense	Suspense	
10			Horror
11			Occult
12	Religion & Spirituality	Occult	
13			Ghosts & Haunted Houses
14		Romance	
15			Paranormal
16			Demons & Devils
17		Science Fiction & Fantasy	
18			Fantasy

So I now have 12 categories in which I could submit my book. Which ones should I choose, because I only can take 2 during my submission on Amazon? The obvious answer is: the 2 that fit the best with your book!

And that depends a lot on your book! Since I haven't really written a book on Dracula or something similar, I have to make some assumptions here. Notice that there are 3 main categories. I decide to take out the "Religion & Spirituality main category (and therefore all its sub-categories). I also take out the "classics" categories, because my book is not a classic (yet).

That leaves me with 6 categories.

We are still analyzing the competition, remember? So let's see how crowded these categories are.

Go onto Amazon into the Kindle Store. Scroll down, till you see the list of main categories.

And I look at the two main categories that I have left in my list:

Literature & Fiction (881,433)

Mystery, Thriller &
Suspense (151,385)

In Literature there are about 6 times more books than in the Mystery category. So in which category it would be the easiest to climb up the ladder? Right, the Mystery one.

Now drill down to the two sub-sub categories under Mystery. What do we see?

‹ Kindle eBooks

‹ Mystery, Thriller & Suspense

Suspense

Ghosts (786)

Horror (2,355)

Occult (840)

Paranormal (1,812)

Political (1,234)

Psychological (10,009)

Same conclusion. The "Occult" category has 3 times less books listed. So it will be easier to get to the top 100 in that one, than if I would start with the horror subcategory.

I do the same analysis for the Literature main category.

Contemporary fiction. 215.773
Horror -> Occult . 14.729
Literary Fiction. 58.977
Mythology & Folk Tales. 18.972

You shouldn't always take the category with the lowest number. It should also fit with your book! But in this case the Horror->Occult category seems a good choice.

So now we have:

Literature & Fiction > Horror > Occult
Mystery, Thriller & Suspense > Suspense > Occult

If possible, always try to find two categories into two different main categories.

Now let's have a look at these two categories and see what the top 100 looks like. I go back to the top of the Kindle eBook store and click on Kindle bestsellers. Now I drill down to the two categories mentioned before. In the Horror section I look at bottom of the list 80-100. Because getting in that list will be the first objective.

I look at a couple of books and look at their Amazon Best Sellers Rank. I see that they all are around #15000. That's a pretty low number, and therefore they are high in sales. (It's like in any top X. The lower the number, the better the book). Somewhere between 5 and 15 copies a day. See for more info Amazon Best Sellers Rank.

Conclusion: It will not be easy to get into that top 100. I do the same for the Mystery Category. And as expected, the bottom of the top 100 is much less crowded. Books rank at 200.000+. So, it will be much easier to get into that top 100.

One last word about categories and the research that I just described. Most authors write a book because they are interested by the topic that they are writing about. But you can also take it the other way around.

Search through the categories to find books that really sell! And then write a book in that category. Or you can apply a mixture of these.

You take a broad category that interests you and then you find the subcategory where there are at least a couple of books that have good sales. As a ballpark figure, you should look for books that have an Amazon Best Sellers Rank of 25.000 or less.

Or put otherwise: If you are going to write a book in a category where the highest ranked books have a Best Sellers Rank of 50.000+ , you can almost be sure that you will never sell more than a couple of copies a day.

There is a lot more to say about analyzing your competition. Especially to analyze what other people say about their books. That might give you some ideas to write about the things that people didn't find in the other books. But all this is part of the process of actually writing your book, which is not the subject of this book.

I might actually write a book on HOW to write a book. :)

- Analyze as much as possible what you can find on these competing books. Who is the author? How many books did they publish? In which categories? What are their reviews like? What is the sales rank of every book? What is the author rank? How many reviews did they get? When were these books published? What did customers say about their books? (This is an interesting exercise, and you will learn how to spot immediately fake or "suspect" reviews. More on this in the chapter reviews)

I will go much deeper into sales rank and author rank later on in this book.

Categories

When you submit your book, you will be asked to specify maximum 2 categories for your book. Now this chapter IS going to be a bit more complicated as the previous ones, because... it is a rather complicated subject.

Actually, on all blogs, forums and books I went through, the most common phrase is "the whole category thing on Amazon is a mess" or something similar. And that's about it.

I gave this a second thought and said to myself: How come that the biggest multi-billion-dollar retailer in the world cannot make this a smooth process? Cannot they pay a programmer for 30 minutes to get this job done? Is this whole thing REALLY a mess? Or is there something behind all this which finally makes a lot of sense?

And my intuition said that there is no such thing as "a mess" on Amazon who is dealing with this stuff already for 20 years now with the smartest developers and marketing people in the world.

So... time to dig into this to figure out how this REALLY works. Why is this important to understand? Because, as I pointed out already in previous chapters, there are THREE things that can make the difference for your book. The cover+title, the keywords and the categories.

So take a cup of coffee, and try to follow this chapter. If you don't grasp it on first read, reread it again. This IS important.

Let's start with what Amazon themselves say about the categories on the submission form:

Here is the short description:

> "A browse category is the section of the Kindle store where users can browse to your book. Think of the browse category like the sections of a physical bookstore (fiction, history, and so on). You can select up to two browse categories for your book. Precise browse categorization helps readers find your book, so identify the most appropriate categories for your book."

Well, that doesn't help us a lot.

On the more extensive help page on Amazon about the choice of categories, we can read the following:

> "There are three main criteria that will help you choose the best   browse   categories.
>
> • **Picking the most accurate categories.** Make sure the categories you've picked correctly describe the subject matter of your book."

That one seems obvious.

*"• **Selecting the most specific categories.** It's better to choose more specific categories instead of more general categories. Customers looking for very specific topics will more easily find your book, and your book will be displayed in more general categories as well (for example, a book in the "FICTION > Fantasy > Historical" category will also show up in searches for general fiction and general fantasy books). You should only select a "General" category if your book is actually a general book about a broad topic."*

The first part is just plain wrong. You CANNOT select a category AND a subcategory of that same category. You can only choose between lowest-level categories. I'll explain that further on.

*"• **Ensuring the categories you choose are not redundant.** Since your book will be displayed in a variety of searches by choosing even a single category, you shouldn't place it in both a category and any of that category's sub-categories (for example, selecting both "FICTION > Fantasy > Historical" and "FICTION > Fantasy"). Even selecting just one specific, accurate category is preferable to selecting an inaccurate category just to have a second category listed."*

This is a repeat of the second point and impossible anyway. The last sentence is correct. But it does imply: IF you can find TWO categories that fit correctly with your book, you should use these two categories. And it is even better if these two subcategories belong to two different main categories. Like the example I described before.

Now let's see how this category selection works in detail. When you come onto the submission page you will see a button "Categories". When you click on it you will get this screen:

Choose categories (up to two):

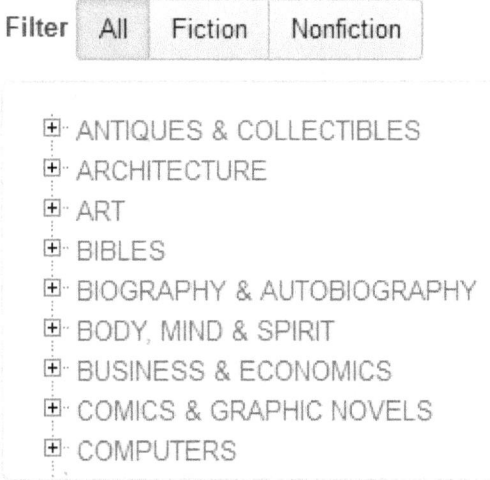

Filter | All | Fiction | Nonfiction

⊞ ANTIQUES & COLLECTIBLES
⊞ ARCHITECTURE
⊞ ART
⊞ BIBLES
⊞ BIOGRAPHY & AUTOBIOGRAPHY
⊞ BODY, MIND & SPIRIT
⊞ BUSINESS & ECONOMICS
⊞ COMICS & GRAPHIC NOVELS
⊞ COMPUTERS

Selected categories:

Choose a category

There are 51 main categories listed here. Now go back to Amazon to the top of the Kindle eBook store. And have a look at the main categories. You will see the following list (it may have changed slightly when you read this).

Arts & Photography

Biographies & Memoirs

Business & Money

Children's eBooks

Comics & Graphic Novels

Computers & Technology

Cookbooks, Food & Wine

Crafts, Hobbies & Home

Education & Reference

Gay & Lesbian

Health, Fitness & Dieting

History

Humor & Entertainment

Literature & Fiction

Mystery, Thriller & Suspense

Nonfiction

Parenting & Relationships

Politics & Social Sciences

Professional & Technical

Religion & Spirituality

Romance

Science & Math

Science Fiction & Fantasy

Self-Help

Sports & Outdoors

Teen & Young Adult

Travel

Foreign Languages

In this list there are 29 main categories. If you look at the first entry in both lists, on the submission form we have "Antiques & Collectibles" and on the Amazon site we have "Arts & Photography".

Yes, the two lists are completely different. And that makes things a bit complicated. Why are these lists different?

The reason is the following: The list that is used on the submission form is the so called BISAC Subject Codes list. This is an international standard that is used by publishing companies to categorize books based on topical content. You can find more on this list over here.

https://www.bisg.org/bisac-subject-codes

This means that this list is NOT maintained and controlled by Amazon, but by an independent organization. And Amazon uses that list because it is an industry standard.

However, the way that Amazon presents books on THEIR site, IS under their control. And the BISAC list is not the best way to browse through a catalog. Amazon has made it in such a way, that there are multiple ways to find a book by a customer who is browsing around.

Let's take an example: On the BISAC list you see the main categories "Juvenile fiction" and "Juvenile non-fiction". Juvenile is a word that isn't used very frequently in the English language and means "intended for young persons". If you develop the "Juvenile Fiction" list you'll see for example:

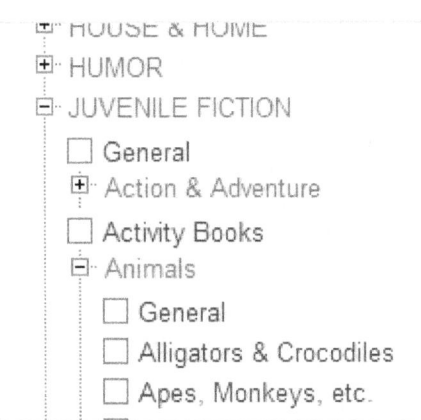

And if I go to the Amazon site and I drill down in the main category "Children's eBooks" I now see the list:

Animals

Alligators & Crocodiles (120)

Apes & Monkeys (465)

Baby Animals (251)

Bears (846)

Birds (1.235)

And here we see the same categories of Animals, Alligators and Monkeys. Conclusion: Amazon is using the term "Children's eBooks" instead of "Juvenile Fiction". And I think they are right from a customer perspective.

So, the only complication for you as an author is to find the two best categories where you want to see your book listed, by using the process that I described before with the Dracula example. And then you have to find in the BISAC submission list the entry that corresponds with it.

For most categories this is not a problem. Because the name and subcategories are the same in both lists. But for others you may have to search a bit. To make this is a bit simpler, I have done the following:

- Expand the BISAC list on the submission form by clicking on all the + symbols. Now I select the whole list and copy and paste it into a spreadsheet. Now it's only a question of some basic formatting to get the complete list of 4246(!) entries.

- The same can be done for the categories on the Amazon site. Select all main categories on the highest level in the Kindle eBook store. Including the number of books in that category. Copy and paste into a spreadsheet. Develop every sub category and repeat. Apply some basic excel formatting and voila. Now I have a complete list of all categories and subcategories with the number of books in each. I only did that for the main categories that I'm writing in, because I don't need all the other thousands.

Now if I have some categories in the Amazon site list, it's quick to use the find function in excel to find the corresponding entry in the BISAC list.

Another way to do this, is to use the site http://browsenodes.com . Without going into the techie details, with this site you can browse through the Amazon category tree, but it is a bit faster than on Amazon. And you can download search trees in CSV format and then import it into excel to analyze it.

I come back to what Amazon writes on their help page and which I qualified as plain wrong. If I develop the BISAC list under Fiction->Fantasy by clicking on the small +symbol in front of the categories, I see the following

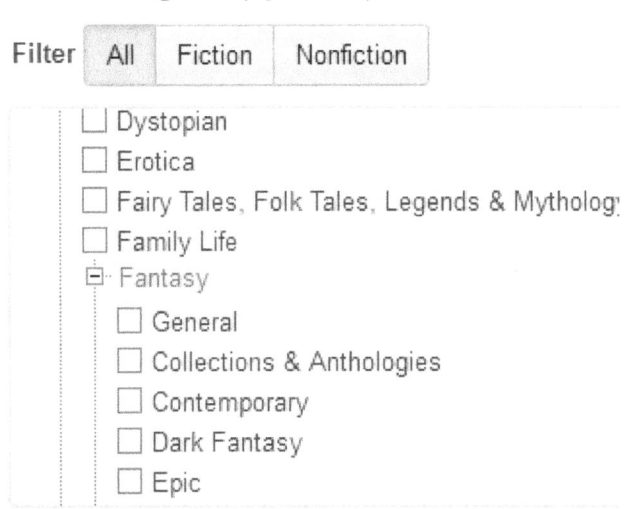

And as you can see, I can only select (=check) boxes that are UNDER "Fantasy". I cannot select the category "Fantasy" as a whole because there is no check box in front of it. So, I can only select the lowest level sub category.

What they MIGHT have meant is that if you select for example the subcategory "Dark Fantasy" don't select also a second category on that same level like "Epic". Rather take another subcategory that is in a completely different main category. Again, as long as it fits with your book.

Why are books listed in the category "Kindle eBooks" and "Books"? Like in this example:

Amazon Best Sellers Rank: #143,279 Paid in Kindle Store (See Top 100 Paid in Kind
   #20 in Kindle Store > Kindle eBooks > Reference > Writing, Research & Publishi
   #60 in Kindle Store > Kindle eBooks > Business & Money > Skills > **Business W**
   #65 in Books > Reference > Writing, Research & Publishing Guides > Writing >

The answer is simple. All eBooks are also part of the bigger category Books. The Books category contains ALL books on Amazon. Hardcopy and eBooks. Therefore, IF your book has a rating in both categories, the rating in the Books category will always be lower, because there are more Books in that category than in the category 'Kindle eBooks'. Also notice, that the category structure under 'Books' is NOT the same as the one under 'eBooks'.

I hope that I have now cleared up this whole issue about category selection.

Formatting your book

Before you publish your book, you should make sure that it is correctly formatted. Formatting errors will probably not prevent a customer from buying your book. However, bad formatting can result in a less than 5-star review or worse. And bad reviews can kill your sales.

You can download a free Kindle formatting guide from Amazon. But it is far from complete. It doesn't explain you in detail how to handle indents, lists, images, Table of Content, non-breaking spaces, headings etc.etc. And if you don't know how to do that you can get into an endless process of uploading and correcting your formatting. That's why I wrote "The Ultimate Kindle Formatting Guide. Better Formatting = More Sales!"

That book describes, in the same level of detail as this book, EVERYTHING you have to know to get a perfectly formatted book. Fiction or non-fiction.

Proofreading

Do you need proofreading for your book? Yes! And preferably by a professional. This means: not just a friend or your neighbor, but someone who has a very good understanding of the language you're writing in and who does writing and proofreading as a profession.

This is also a task that you can outsource on the internet, on sites like fiverr.com, odesk.com and freelance.com . Count approximately $5-$10 per 1000 words for proofreading.

This of course, after you have proofread your whole document yourself, for at least 3 times. The last time, reading it out loud.

Prepare a submission file

Now that you have your eBook ready for publishing, you are going to upload it to Amazon. Read the Kindle formatting guide, or my book, how to prepare that in the right format with htm and zip files.

Before starting the upload and creating your book on Amazon, it may be handy to create a book submission file. You use this file to fill out quickly all the information that is required when submitting a book.

And because it is likely that you are going to submit similar information on other sites to promote your book, it is handy to have all this info in one file. Create this file with notepad and type in the following information in plain text:

• The title

• The subtitle

• The description of the book. Maximum 4000 characters. But don't overdo it. This is the description that will show up under your book. No one is going to read 10 pages of a book description. Keep it in a couple of paragraphs. You can use certain HTML codes in this description **on Amazon**. On other sites, the description field should be plain text without HTML codes.

  The full list of HTML codes that you can use on Amazon in the description is here:

  https://kdp.amazon.com/help?topicId=A377RPHW6ZG4D8

  So you could put in the description field for example:

  This is my Title in bold

And this text in your description would come out in bold.

You want to include a bullet list in your description? Here is how to do it:

```
<ul>
<li> This is my first bullet item</li>
<li>This is my second bullet item</li>
</ul>
```

The 'u' stands for 'unordered'
You want it numbered? No problem. Do it as follows:

```
<ol>
<li> This is my first numbered item</li>
<li>This is my second numbered item</li>
</ol>
```

The 'o' stands for 'ordered'.

But I noticed that some work, and others don't. So again, keep it simple. Don't put all kinds of fancy color codes or heading codes in there. They may NOT work.

- The author or authors

- The link to your book on Amazon. You don't have that one yet, but you will get one as soon as your book is published. So the sequence is: publish your book, get the ASIN number, include the link in your book so that the link for reviews works correctly, and republish your book. If you use a Pretty Link or Bitly, you don't have to do this. As soon as you have your ASIN, you just create your Pretty or Bitly link.

When you are going to submit your book to other sites to promote it, these sites will ask for your Amazon link. As I explain in the chapter about tracking codes, you would typically use a pretty link for all sites where you are going to submit your book.

- An excerpt: This is a shorter description (max 400 words) that you may be required to fill in on other sites for book submission.

- The categories. I have covered these extensively.

- The keywords.

- Your author profile. You create a profile to be published on your Amazon Central Author page. In your submission file you include the same profile, and the link to that profile on Amazon. More on Author Central further on.

The procedure for this link to your Author profile is the same as for your book. As soon as you have published your book, you can fill out your author profile. Now you have your link to your author profile, for those submission sites that will ask for that link.

- Your cover image in a separate file.

- The language of your book.

- DRM. When you submit your book to Amazon, you have to decide if you want DRM applied to your book. This is a protection mechanism to protect your book. I write more about piracy and protection in the chapter Piracy. If you're not sure, select NO DRM. Because IF you apply DRM protection you cannot undo it. But you can always apply it later on. I suggest that you select DRM enabled.

When you have finished with this submission file there are still a couple of details that you have to think about. One of them is... the price!

Price

It shouldn't come as a surprise that the price of your book is an important factor in the final sales results for your book. And normally, as with a lot of products you might expect: The higher your sales price, the less you will sell. Well, actually that is not true.

Here is an interesting chart from Smashwords. This data is collected over 120.000 sales so we can consider it as representative. (Notice that charts on other sites seem to confirm the conclusions of this one).

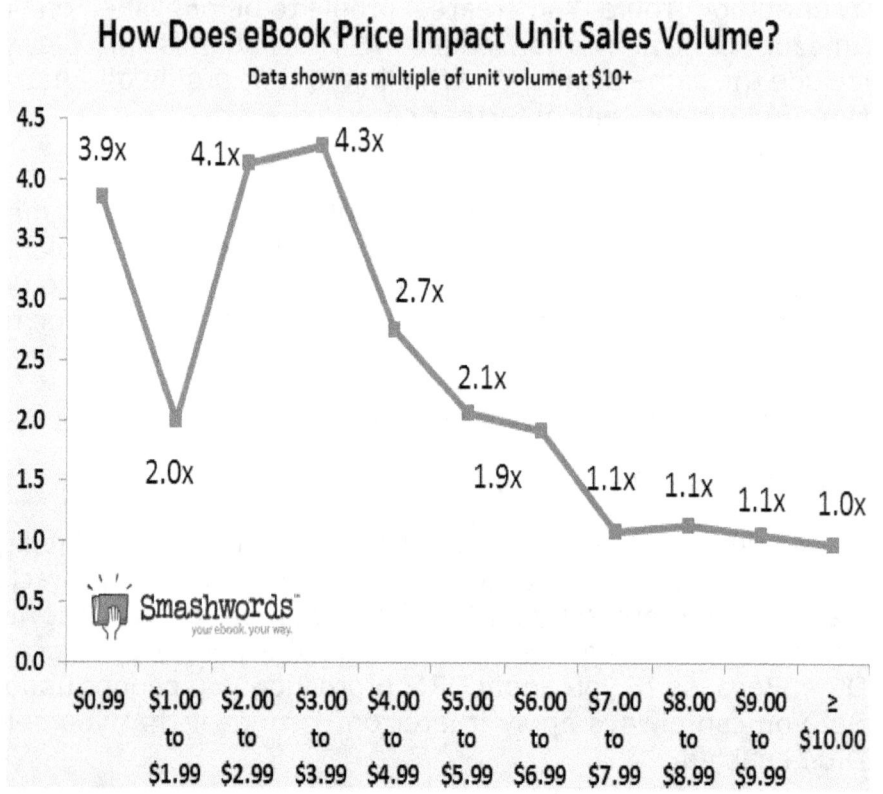

- At $0.99 sales are almost 4x higher than at $10.

- Between $1.00 and $1.99 there is a black hole. So authors either go for the real low point of $0.99 or at the higher price point between $2.99 and $3.99.

- From 3.99 onwards the traditional formula, higher price->fewer sales is confirmed. Note that selling fewer copies doesn't always mean making less income. When you increase the price of your book with 10% and your sales go down with 5% you still make more money than with the lower price. There is an optimal point, where an increase of X% in your price will result in X%+ less sales. The only way to find out that optimal price point is by trial and error.

To set the price of your book, it is imperative to study the prices of your competitors. Prices of most non-fiction books are under $5.

The best price for your book is...FREE. On average, when a book is offered for free, the download numbers are approximately 90-100x higher then when they are for sale.

Calculated over all books and categories, the best price point seems to be $3.99.

Certain authors argue that their work deserves more than $2.99 or $3.99. In this game, like any business, it is the customer that votes with his wallet. Don't get carried away with what YOU think your book is worth. What's important is what your customers think it is worth.

Lowering your price doesn't mean necessarily that your total income will go down. First, you will sell more units, so you will have more exposure. And that might mean other valuable things. More subscribers to your list, more visitors to your site.

Also notice that there is a low point where potential customers will find your book to "cheap" to be credible. Lots of case studies have proven that increasing your sales point from a very low price might actually INCREASE the number of units sold.

Let's extend a bit on the FREE price. Sure, if you offer your book for free, you will not make any direct income with it. But you shouldn't consider these free downloads as missed sales. There are multiple advantages of giving away your book for 2 or 3 days.

- Exposure. More downloads mean more potential customers. Not for this book, but maybe for the next.

- Every free download may lead to some other sales on Amazon, IF you send them there through your affiliate link

- When people download your free book, and they like it, they may have a look at other books you have written.

- "Giving away" 1000 or 2000 copies is peanuts on the millions of potential customers. Don't see it as lost sales but purely as a promotion. Like a shop that opens and organizes an open day with free snacks and drinks. This is your promotion. Not giving away products for nothing.

- A lot of people that download free copies during a promotion are just freebie seekers. They would never have bought your book regardless the price. So, you shouldn't consider them as "lost sales".

Royalties

I will remain very short on this one. Royalties will be 35% if your book is priced less than $2.99 and 70% from $2.99 onwards. For all details, visit the Amazon Pricing Page

Delivery costs

Just a couple of words on delivery costs. Yes, although your eBook will be delivered electronically, Amazon still counts delivery costs for your eBook. These depend on the size of your eBook. It's roughly $0.15 ct/Megabyte . And if you're writing novels, you can put 1.000.000 characters in a Megabyte. So you don't have to worry too much about these couple of cents for delivery.

However, if you're writing a book about photography with lots of high-resolution pictures or screen captures, the delivery cost may go up significantly.

Imagine your book is 2 Mb in size. That's $0,30 cts on delivery costs. If your book is priced at 3.69 on Amazon, the book price that will be used for the calculation of your royalties will be the 3.69 minus VAT. This depends a bit on the country you live in. But let's say that the net royalty price is $3.29.

Of this $3.29, you get 70%, which is $2.30. And now, your delivery costs are 0.30/2.30 = 13% of these royalties!!

So be sure that you compress images as much as possible. Or even better, resize and compress them before you publish your book.

The size that is taken into account for this calculation is NOT the size of your MOBI file, neither the size of the zip file you upload, nor the file size that is shown on the detail page of your book. The size of the file that is taken into account is mentioned on the bottom of the pricing table when you submit your file.

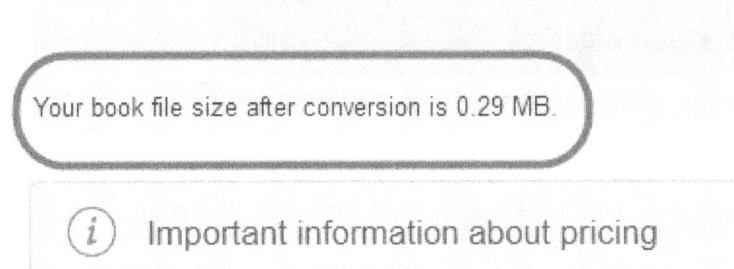

Your book file size after conversion is 0.29 MB.

(i) Important information about pricing

Tip: If you use Word to write your book, uncheck the tick box "Allow PNG as a graphics format" under Word Options->Advanced->Web Options. This will result in a slightly smaller file on Amazon. Or even better: convert all your images to GIF format.

Publish your book

Now that you have everything ready, you can go to the submission page on Amazon and publish your book. This is a rather straight forward process if you have gone through the previous preparation steps. Fill out the first form that asks you for title, keywords, cover, content file etc. Do verify that you don't have any formatting errors. Verify again all links. (See my formatting book for more details).

When that's ok, click 'Save and Publish'. You will now go the second page of the submission process where you will be asked for the price and royalties option.

If you have still some doubts, you can save everything here as a draft. But if everything is ok, click "Save and Publish". Your book will be available on Amazon within a couple of hours and you will be notified by email. Now you have your Amazon ASIN number.

Don't start immediately a KDP select promotion, because that requires some preparation and that's what the rest of this pre-launch chapter is all about.

When you submit your book on Amazon, you can check of the box if you want to participate in the KDP Select program. You don't have to make up your mind immediately. You can always submit your book without the KDP Select option and activate it later on.

What is KDP Select?

KDP Select (Kindle Direct Publishing Select) is an optional program on Amazon that makes your book eligible for certain promotional tools on Amazon. If you use these tools, your books will get more exposure and therefore you may expect more sales.

In exchange for being able to use these tools, you will have to give exclusivity for your book to Amazon. This means that you can sell your book ONLY on Amazon. Not on other platforms (Smashwords, iBookstore, B&N etc.), not on your own site, not on a friend's site. Nowhere. You cannot even give it away for free, other than through the Amazon platform.

The moment you enroll your book in KDP Select you engage yourself for a 90-day period. You CAN un-publish your book from the KDP Select program at any time during this 90-day period, but the exclusivity right will continue for the full 90 days. In other words, if you un-publish your book from KDP Select, you cannot make it available through any other platform (for sale or free), until the 90-day period expires.

Renewal will be automatic at the end of the 90-day period unless you state otherwise.

What are the major benefits of KDP select?

When you give exclusivity for your book to Amazon, you can use two promotion tools that are not at your disposal when your book is not part of KDP select.

1. **FREE promotions**: You get the privilege to give away your book for free by using the "KDP Free promotion" option. Yes, this may sound a bit strange, but giving your book away for a certain number of days can help your sales AFTER the free period.

Now I know that certain authors do not agree AT ALL, with this "give away" strategy. As an illustration, I'll post here an extract of a forum post, in which I had a discussion with someone about giving your book away for free or not.

"(...) you are experiencing the high of seeing your book in print and getting into people's hands. Very exciting. And so, in a way, your thinking and reaction is on par with a fifth grader who has sold his first 30 boxes of Christmas wrapping paper, netting a whole $4 per each, and a whopping $150. Very exciting money if you are ten years of age.

However, if you are in a community of adults serious about making a living on writing, $150 stinks. What mortgage can you pay today with that money? (...) How about none.

So we really have to stop thinking along the lines of the conditioning going on also in the author community to get giddy on giving your hard earned work away and to make 30, 40 whatever in results, see the high of the stats in your book's placement, and see some little stars in your reviews. Instead we have to break out of that hypnosis and think real numbers and returns and stop treating our books as school projects and club projects, getting giddy over deceptive figures.

(...)
I wish there was a way to de-condition this mind frame that makes all people want to break out the champagne after throwing away large numbers of their eBooks and getting deceptively small sales in return, deceptive in that they have no real-world financial punch and no lasting impact beyond the freebie giveaway period until it vaporizes with the next author's freebie bash making yours yesterday's long lost news.

(...) I, too, almost bit that bait, until I looked and looked and looked to data just in the last few weeks and started reading

all the regrets from authors who netted zilch or they had dismal returns comparing to a couple years ago on another freebie, or my own seeing that eBooks now are all priced like they are less valuable than comic books were ten years ago. This shouldn't be, and we should not be blinded by the high of a few sales and many free downloads. It is a deception. (...)"

I guess that it is clear that this person wants to get paid for her books what she thinks is a fair price. And that's her good right.

My take is that your book is worth what a customer wants to give for it.

So, should you participate in KDP select? I'm not going to give you any advice on this one. But let me give you another point of view. If Amazon asks you a favor (exclusivity) in exchange for something else (free book promotion), you can be sure that this feature has value and wasn't pulled out of a hat on a rainy Friday afternoon. The whole point of these marketing tricks from Amazon is that YOU make more sales. Because if YOU make more sales, they also earn more money.

If KDP select wasn't working for authors, it would have been replaced with something else by Amazon already a long time ago. You make your own conclusions.

The sure way to find out, is to put your book in KDP Select and another one NOT in KDP select, and compare the difference.

Here are some details about the KDP Select "Free promotion" option. During the 90-day period, you get 5 days to promote your book for free. You can use these 5 days as you wish. 5 times 1 day every 2 weeks. Or one period of 3 days followed later on with a period of 2 days. Or whatever you want to do with these 5 days. Up to you.

Most authors use these 5 days as follows: 2 or 3 days when they launch their book. 1 day is too short to create momentum. It's like the gearbox of a car. To get up to a reasonable speed, you first put it in 1st gear, then 2nd and finally in 3rd. If you take your foot of the accelerator after just having passed 1st gear, you won't have made any high speed yet.

Then, a couple of weeks later, you can use the remaining 2 days.

Statistically the Sunday and Monday are the days of the week with the highest sales on Amazon. You might take this into an account when you plan your KDP Select Free promotion.

Depending on the number of days of your promotion, you would choose the following days:

5 days: Saturday-Wednesday.

4 days: Sunday-Wednesday

3 days: Sunday-Tuesday

2 days: Sunday-Monday

1 day: Monday

2. **Kindle Countdown deals**. This is the second promotion tool that you can use if your book is enrolled into KDP Select. Notice that during a 90-day enrollment period, you can use EITHER the free promotion OR the Countdown deal.

   There are a number of prerequisites before you are allowed to use the Countdown deal promotion tool.

   • Your book should be at least already for 30 days into the KDP select program.

   • The regular price has not been changed during the last 30 days. And you are not allowed to change it for 14 days AFTER the end of the Countdown deal.

   • The regular price should be $2.99 or higher.

When your book fulfils these requirements, you can setup your Countdown deal. This means that you define a start price, a start date/time, an increment price (min $1) and a duration (max 7 days).

Example: on day 1 start with $0.99. On day 3 increment to $1.99. On day 5 increment to $2.99. At the end, on day 7, increment to the regular price of $3.99.

Look at the free promotion as a booster of a rocket. It will put your eBook into the right orbit. When your eBook is already for some time on sale, but you see that it's getting down a bit in its orbit, use a countdown deal to rectify the orbit.

One drawback of a free promotion is that your book is not for sale anymore. Now that doesn't make any difference when you launch a new book. But when you do a free promotion on a book that is already for several months published and which has a good sales rank, when you do a FREE promotion, your sales will stop and its ranking will go down. That's another reason why you should rather use a countdown deal than a free promotion after a couple of months.

Lending and Borrowing Books

Although lending and borrowing books is marginal on Amazon, I resume here in a couple of words what this is all about and what it means for you as an author.

On Amazon there are two separate things concerning lending and borrowing:

• Kindle Owners' Lending Library (KOLL). When you enroll in KDP select your book will participate in the KOLL program. This means that customers can borrow your book under certain conditions. For every borrow you will get a compensation. But not the same amount as a normal sale. The amount you will get for your borrows is calculated as follows.

Every month, Amazon sets aside an amount that will be distributed between all titles that will be borrowed for the next month. Your share will be calculated as the number of borrows of your title(s) against the total number of all borrows that month on Amazon.

Example: Amazon sets aside $1.000.000 for month X. This amount varies every month. It is announced every month on the KDP select site and the KDP community in the Announcements section. During the next month in total there will be 300.000 borrows on Amazon. You had 10 of these. You will receive 10/300.000= 0.000033 or 0.0033% of 1.000.000 which makes.... $33.33.

- Lending for Kindle. This means that any customer that **has purchased** your book can lend it out for 14 days to a friend of family. Of course, you will get the royalties as a normal sale from the customer that bought the book. But you will get nothing from the lending to his friend.

All books that participate in KDP Select will be enrolled in this lending program automatically. But you may choose to opt-out of this by un-checking the box "Kindle Book Lending" when you submit your book.

Prepare a landing page

If you have a website, you should create a dedicated landing page for your book on your site. On this page, you explain the solution that your book offers to the problem the customer may have (for a non-fiction book). You will use this landing page to send visitors from your landing page to Amazon. For example for a Facebook campaign. Notice that Amazon doesn't allow you to send Facebook traffic (CPM or CPC) or any other paid traffic, directly to their site. Here is the extract from the Amazon T & C's on paid traffic.

*"**Prohibited Paid Search Placement** means an advertisement that you purchased through bidding on keywords, search terms, or other identifiers (including Proprietary Terms) or other participation in keyword auctions. "**Proprietary Term**" means keywords, search terms, or other identifiers that include the word "amazon," "Kindle," "myhabit," or "Javari," or any other trademark of Amazon or its affiliates or variations or misspellings of any of those words (e.g., "ammazon," "amaozn," "kindel," and "javary"). "**Redirecting Link**" means a link that sends users indirectly to the Amazon Site via an intermediate site or webpage and without requiring the user to click on a link or take some other affirmative action on that intermediate site or webpage. "**Search Engine**" means Google, Yahoo, Bing, or any other search engine, portal, sponsored advertising service, or other search or referral service, or any site that participates in any of their respective networks."*

Setup Tracking codes.

Before I start this chapter, let me first say that what I'm going to describe here is important for the rest of your publishing career. But it is not crucial to have all of this in place right from day 1. I mean, if in the first month of your publishing career you make 50 sales, yes, they will not be included in the reporting that we're going to setup now. But don't worry too much about that. The point is that you have to set this up some moment in time to understand what is going on. (If you want to know what works and what not).

In the next chapter I will discuss a lot of things you can do to give your book more visibility by promoting it. Free book sites, YouTube, Facebook etc.etc. But how do you know that these things will actually get you some results? And which actions gave the best results? Would be interesting to know, not? I mean, I you have taken 10 actions, and in the results it turns out that, measured as a result of your overall sales, the numbers are as follows:

• Action 1. 40% of the results

• Action 2. 30% of the results

- Action 3. 20% of the results

- Action 4 to action 10: together 10% of the results.

If would be clear where to put your subsequent marketing efforts for your book and probably also the next titles that you're going to write.

That's what's called the conversion rate of your marketing strategies.

Notice that the above percentages are expressed as a percentage of YOUR efforts. Not of what Amazon is bringing in. Because what's going on on Amazon, that's almost impossible to track. If you're confused now, please bear with me. I think everything will become crystal clear when you go through this whole chapter.

First question: How are you going to know, how many people that you drove from a Facebook campaign, resulted in a sale? And how many from your Twitter messages? And how many from your YouTube trailer?

Now there are all kinds of sophisticated (and expensive) packages to follow all of that. Hitsniffer, Clicktale, Crazyegg, Clicky, Kissmetrics, Google analytics. The problem is that you can track just about anything what is going on on YOUR site, because you can fiddle around on your own site with whatever you like. But here we are talking about a database that is NOT under your complete control. The one from Amazon. So why not use Amazon's reporting capabilities to get that data?

What we are going to use is: Tracking codes through your Amazon affiliate account. Because, the only way to find out from Amazon where visitors that bought your book came from is by using an Amazon affiliate account. And it is FREE. Or even better, you get paid for it!! I'll get to that later on.

Huh? I hear some authors now thinking: "Do I have to get into affiliate marketing to get some data? I'm an author! " Keep cool.

This all sounds probably more complex than it actually is. First let me paint the overall picture.

Suppose you decide to setup a 1-minute video trailer on YouTube for your book. In (or under) that video, you put a link that points to your book on Amazon, right?

Suppose that you use an affiliate link. Something like

www.amazon.com/This_link_comes_from_my_youtube_video/The_book_is_Great_Marketing/The_Author_is_Timo_Hofstee.

The nitty-gritty details will be a bit different, but you get the idea.

If you have an Amazon affiliate account, and you send someone with that affiliate link to your book, in your reporting from Amazon you will get something like:

"Sales made from the traffic you send us from YouTube: 100 clicks, 5 sales."

You also could have used a straight, simple, plain link to your book on Amazon. The one you get when you publish your book. Something like:

www.amazon.com/some-codes/bookname.

If you had used THAT link from your YouTube trailer to your book, these 5 sales would just be reported by Amazon in the "Total sales for your book: 100". And you would have no clue if in that figure, there were 2 or 5 or 30 made through your YouTube promotion.

Got the difference?

IF in your Amazon report it would come out as "Sales from your YouTube video: 1000 clicks, 0 sales", you would have a good indication what you would do with your YouTube videos for your next title. No?

Good. Now that we have established that you need an Amazon affiliate account, how are we going to set that up?

Go to the Amazon Associates Program and click on join. They will ask you for your website. Don't know why, because you could use affiliate links without having a website. But you will need one anyway sooner or later. So just set a very basic one up using Wordpress if you don't have a website yet. How to do this is out of the scope of this book. But setting up a basic standard Wordpress site shouldn't take you more than 2 hours.

When you have gone through the affiliate setup (5 minutes), you will get some affiliate code like "yoursite-20". We're not going to use that one. Now we are going to create tracking codes for all your activities. Here's how I do this:

• Create a new spreadsheet.

• Create the columns as shown in this example:

Book		Media		campaign description		Tracking code
Book Title	Book title code	Media title	Media title code	campaign description	campaign code	
150 Ways	150w	From the auth	ftau	xxx	xxx	150wftauxxx
	150w	List	elst	Free download	fdl	150welstfdl
	150w	YouTube	ytub	video trailer 1	vt1	150wytubvt1

The Book Title column is obvious. The media title column contains the media that I'm using for a marketing activity. Twitter, Facebook, email list etc. The campaign column contains a description what I'm going to do on that media. For example: free promo to email list or paid promo to my email.

For every three of these columns, I create a 3 or 4 letter abbreviation. You can take whatever you like. In the tracking code column, I just use the formula =CONCATENATE (), which glues the 3 abbreviated columns into one tracking code.

I also have a "Used" column with 1/0 (not shown). That indicates if I have actually used that code or not. That's important to track, because if you don't see any results in your sales report for a specific tracking code, it's useful to know if you have actually used it or not. :)

Yes, these codes can quickly add up. If you have 15 marketing activities for 5 books, that's 75 codes. But you don't have to create and use them all immediately. Note that you can create maximum 100 tracking ID's. If you need more, you have to contact Amazon. And don't overdo it. If you post your book on 10 free-book sites for promotion, don't use a different code for every site. Just use one code for all sites. If this turns out to be a good strategy, you can always drill down with more specific codes.

Note also that you CANNOT delete tracking codes!

Next step is, to create these codes on Amazon. Here is how to do this. Log into your affiliate account. (Go to the same page as mentioned before and login with your Amazon account credentials).

On the top left you will see your affiliate code that you got from Amazon when you created your affiliate account.

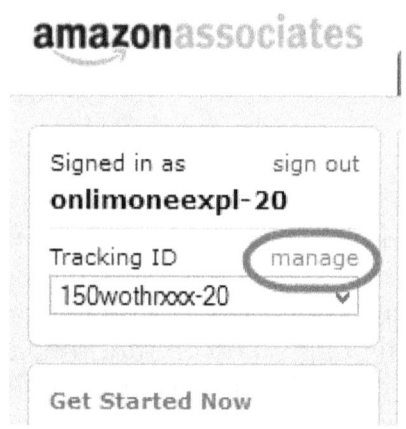

Now click on "manage" to create a new tracking code. On the next screen click on "Add Tracking ID". Copy and paste one of your tracking codes out of your spreadsheet into the form that comes up.

In my case, for my video trailer to my book "The Ultimate Kindle Formatting Guide" I use the code ukmgytubvt1. Click on search. Amazon will check if your code is unique amongst all the affiliate codes used. I never ran into the situation that it wasn't. Click on Create. Done! Note that during the creation process of the tracking id, Amazon will add some other characters to the end. In my case "-20".

Now you have to link that code to your book. I show you how to do that with my code ukmgytubvt1. First, I select that code on the left top of the screen from the drop-down list.

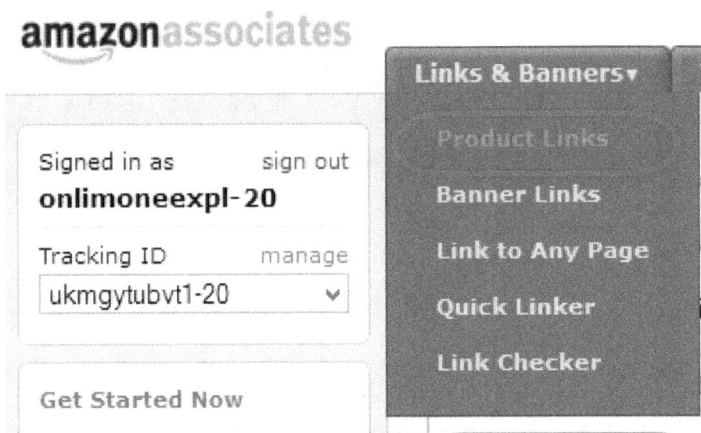

I click on "Links & Banners" and select "Product Links". Now I have to find my book in the search form that comes up. I just copy and paste the ASIN number of my book, which I have open in another tab.

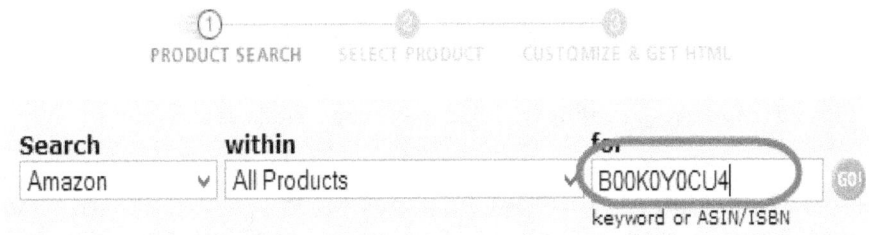

And click "Go!". When your book comes up, click on "Get link"

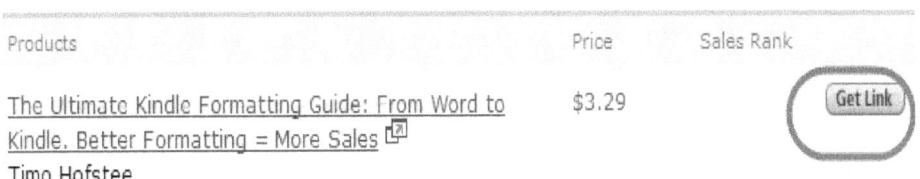

A page is shown with all possible links (Text, Image, Text+image, widget). Click on "Text Only".

Build a link to a specific page from Amazon using the tool

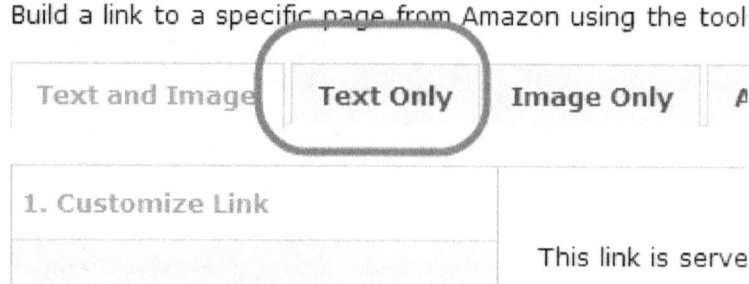

You now will see some HTML code out of which you have to copy the part that is between double quotes " ". (The blue part in the next screen shot).

You now will see some HTML code out of which you have to copy the part that is between double quotes " ". (The blue part in the next screen shot).

Select that piece, CTRL+C (copy) and paste it into your spreadsheet in a new column "Amazon Link". You're done with Amazon. This all seems very lengthy, but if you have done 2 it will take you seconds to create the next ones.

Now there is one small problem left. The URL that you just copied and pasted is rather long. In the example above 168 characters. So suppose that you have gone through the same process to create a link that you are going to use in your Twitter messages. These are max 140 characters. Therefore using this very long URL is not going to work. What you need is a way to shorten that link.

There are two popular ways to do that: Bitly and Pretty Link. (There are more but I will only discuss these popular and free ones).

Bitly: See bitly.com. You give it a long URL like the one above and it will give you a unique, but much shorter link back that you can then use instead of the very long one. Something like http://bit.ly/1juHI4r.

Now every time someone clicks on that short link it behaves as if the user had clicked on your long URL link to Amazon. Additional benefit: Bitly will record all those clicks and then you can make all kinds of nice graphs out of these. The disadvantage is that these clicks don't pass through your site (if you have one).

That's why I prefer:

Pretty Link: This is a free plug-in that you install on your Wordpress site. The principle is the same as Bitly. You give it a long URL and YOU specify the short code or name that you want to use for it. In the example above, I would take the long URL that I got from Amazon and create a short link like http://onlinemoneyexplained.com/ukmgytubvt1. The last characters are the code that I made up in my spreadsheet for my YouTube promotion.

Yes, a bit longer than Bitly, but now, every time that someone clicks on that link it also gets accounted for as traffic to my site. For the rest it works the same. The user will finally end up on my book on Amazon through my affiliate link. And Pretty Link has also some reporting facilities build in.

I'm not going to show here in detail how to create a Pretty Link on your website because that is very straight-forward. Install the plug-in, click on "New Pretty link", paste in the long URL that you got from Amazon, paste in the code that you came up with in your spreadsheet and done!

Now you are ready to use this code in your promotion efforts. In this example, I go to YouTube, post my video and I post the link onlinemoneyexplained/ukmgytubvt1. In this specific case, where your link is visible to the audience, you may decide to create a SECOND Pretty Link to your book, using a more memorable name. For example:

OnlineMoneyExplained.com/Kindle_Formatting, which also points to the same very long URL that I got from Amazon.

Ok. Done!! And now, when you get your reports from Amazon you will see:

Tracking ID: ukmgytubvt1. 100 clicks. 5 sales.

And you put that data into a nice reporting spreadsheet, which now enables you to analyze all this by media, by book, by campaign, etc.etc.

Repeat for all your tracking codes, books and campaigns, and after a couple of weeks/months you have a nice spreadsheet to analyze what is going on exactly. And what works and what not.

Ahh, I told you that you will even make some money with this. Ok, let me explain.

You have just setup yourself an Amazon affiliate tracking account for tracking the sales of your book in detail. Right? But it IS a full Amazon affiliate account. This means a couple of things:

- When you sell one of your books, you will of course get paid for the sale of that book, but you will ALSO get 4% on top of that, because you made that sale as an affiliate. For Amazon, it's "just a sale" that you have made by referring someone to "a product" on their site. It just happens to be your own book. 4% , that's a whopping $0,13 ct for every sale. Big deal. But when you get to selling a couple of hundred a month, it's a nice bonus. But things even get better...

- When you send someone through your affiliate link to Amazon, you will get 4% (minimum) on ANYTHING that this person buys on Amazon within the next 24 hours! So, imagine this scenario: You send someone to Amazon for your book, but it doesn't result in a sale. Instead, he buys a book from your competitor. You will get 4% on that sale!

And it gets even better: imagine that you have written a book on fitness equipment. And you send someone with your affiliate link to Amazon to your book. The customer buys your book. Reads the book and orders 10 hours later an $800 treadmill on Amazon. You get 4% on that one also! That's $32. And that's just free bonus on top of your nice reports.

With a bit of luck, just promoting your books with your affiliate link instead of using plain, straight forward links, will make you enough to pay for your hosting, auto responder and all the rest of it. Just as a bonus. And this holds also for your FREE promotions.

Imagine you do a free KDP select promotion which you announce all over the place and you get 2000 free downloads. That's good for your marketing. But... out of these 2000 free downloads, maybe 10 customers will keep hanging around on Amazon and buy something else. Makeup, clothes, books or whatever. You get 4% of that. Maybe you can even make more money from your free promotions then with your regular sales. :)

Author Central

When you have published your book, you can create an Author page on Author Central. This will be mentioned in the mail that you get from Amazon as soon as your book is published.

Fill out your Author Central page. Write something about yourself. Why you write, who you are, where you live, your hobbies. Maybe people want to know more about you. What you fill in on your Author page will appear under the detail of your books in the "About the author" section.

On your Author Central page, you can fill out lots of other things.

• Photos.

• Your website.

• Your RSS feed.

• Videos of interviews, book trailers.

• Create a dedicated link to your Author Central page. You can then use that link to put on your website, mail signature, business cards etc.

• Your Twitter account

• Events like: book signatures, presentations etc.

Important: When you create your Author page on amazon.com it will NOT be used automatically on all the other Amazon sites. Makes sense, because on amazon.fr you would like to have your Author page in French and on amazon.de in German.

Therefore, if you sell your book worldwide, you would have to go, to the page http://authorcentral.amazon.fr to fill out your Author page in French. The same for the other Amazon sites. At this moment there are the following Amazon sites with an Author central page:

• amazon.com . US

• amazon.de . Germany

• amazon.fr. France

• amazon.co.uk . UK

If you haven't created an Author Central page for any of these sites, and the user clicks on your Author profile, he will just get a listing of your books. The same is true for Amazon sites where there is no Author central, like amazon.it (Italy).

Notice that when you publish your eBook worldwide, it will be available on 12 out of the 13 Amazon websites. These are:

• amazon.com : US

• amazon.in : India

• amazon.de : Germany

• amazon.co.uk : UK

• amazon.fr : France

• amazon.es : Spain

• amazon.it : Italy

• amazon.co.jp : Japan

• amazon.ca : Canada

• amazon.com.mx : Mexico

- amazon.com : Australia

- amazon.com.br : Brazil

The only site where you cannot publish your eBook (yet) is amazon.cn or z.cn (China). You can only publish a hardcopy of your book on this site.

When you have finished with filling out your author profile, you can go to your book from the author central page. And you can fill in even more information about your book, like

- Editorial reviews. From the Inside Flap. From the Backcover.

- Book extras. This is information like : Characters, synopsis, quotations, awards etc. To modify this data, you have to go to the site shelfari and fill out these details. They will then appear also on Amazon. (Shelfari is owned by Amazon).

Your Amazon profile page

When you participate in the Amazon communities, you do so with your Amazon profile. This profile is different from your author profile. To edit your Amazon profile, click on 'Your Account' on the top right of any Amazon page, scroll down to the 'Personalization' section and select 'Your Public Profile'.

Guides:

You can create so called "So You'd Like To..." guides. So for example, you could write a guide "So You'd Like To Sell More Kindle eBooks".

The whole idea here, again, is to write a guide with keywords that will be indexed by the search engines. When people search for those keywords they may get directed to your guide, and finally to your books.

For more information about these guides go here.

Schedule your KDP select promotion

Now that your book is published you are going to schedule your KDP Select promotion. Go to your bookshelf, click on your book and click on KDP select. You now have the choice between running a free promotion period or a countdown deal. Note that to use the countdown deal, your book has to be published already at least for 30 days. And during the 90-day KDP Select period you can only use one OR the other.

Spread the word

Now that you have published your book and scheduled your promotion, you should spread the word about the book. Note that these activities should be done 1 or 2 weeks BEFORE the actual launch day. This is the day that your KDP select promotion will start.

You are going to announce on a lot of places: "My book will be available for free from date X to date Y". Or "From date X onwards I will run a countdown deal on my book ABC".

I have split up the categories where you can promote your book in 5 main chapters:

• Twitter

• Facebook

• Free submission websites.

• Your website

• Other

Now there are literally HUNDREDS of places where you can promote your book for free or paid. And if you would want to use ALL of these, you will be busy for a while. There are several ways to speed up this whole process:

• Outsource it to someone else

• Use aggregation software. Popular ones are HootSuite and Gremln. These sites function as a sort of central dashboard for all your Twitter, FaceBook, Google+ and other social media accounts.

Prepare a message that you're going to tweet. Something like: "My new book 'Title' will be available for FREE download from x to y. Link" . In which link is the link that you prepared as described in the chapter Setup Tracking Codes.

First you can tweet it of course to all your followers.

Next you can search for twitter accounts that deal with free eBook promotion. For example, when I type into the Twitter search box for "Kindle", "eBook", "free book" etc. I find dozens of accounts. Examples are:

- https://twitter.com/freedailybooks

- https://twitter.com/goodreads

- https://twitter.com/kindleeBooks

- https://twitter.com/BookBub

- https://twitter.com/PixelofInk

- https://twitter.com/fkbt

- https://twitter.com/FreeeBooksDaily

- https://twitter.com/FreeBooksUK

- https://twitter.com/KindleFreeReads

- https://twitter.com/KindleToday

- https://twitter.com/kindlefreeBook

- https://twitter.com/Kindle_FREE

- https://twitter.com/IndieKindle

- https://twitter.com/KindleFireGuide

- https://twitter.com/free2kindle

- https://twitter.com/Goodkindles

You can also use twellow.com to find quickly more of these.

Next you can try to find people that have the problem that you address in your non-fiction book. For example, if your book is about "stop smoking", you can search on twitter for accounts that tweet about this problem and include them in your tweet list.

Facebook

Prepare a similar message as for Twitter, but now including your link with the Facebook free promo tracking code.

First you can post it of course on your own personal page and your Fan Page.

Next, you can search for kindle groups on FB and post the promotion message in these groups. Make sure that you ALWAYS read the rules first for every group. Some allow you to only post in specific threads.

You can find those kinds of groups by using the same predictive search function as described for Amazon (or Google). For example, type in just "Kindle" in the search box on the top of your page without pressing ENTER. I now get:

Kindle|

Pat's First Kindle Book (From Sta
Closed Group · 6,459 members

Awesome Free Kindle Books Her
Closed Group · 8,357 members

The Kindle Publishing Bible
Closed Group · 2,737 members

free kindle and nook ebooks for
Closed Group · 12,322 members

Free Today on Kindle & Beyond
Open Group · 6,062 members

Free Kindle Books
Open Group · 8,876 members

Kindle Publishers
Open Group · 4,333 members

 Find all groups named "Kindle"

Now you can become a member of those groups, or find more groups by clicking on the last box "Find all groups". You can repeat this with keywords like: Free Book, eBook etc. Here are a couple of Facebook groups that you can start with. But again, there are dozens and dozens of these.

- https://www.faceBook.com/groups/294455560643884/

- https://www.faceBook.com/groups/293618244055941/

- https://www.faceBook.com/groups/204725947524/

- https://www.faceBook.com/groups/freetoday/

- https://www.faceBook.com/groups/freebkrus/

- https://www.faceBook.com/groups/freeeBooks/

- https://www.faceBook.com/groups/270558336379692/

- https://www.faceBook.com/groups/FreeTodayOnAmazon/

- https://www.faceBook.com/groups/179494068820033/

- https://www.faceBook.com/groups/borntowrite/

- https://www.faceBook.com/groups/apablog/

- https://www.faceBook.com/groups/370900356880/

- https://www.faceBook.com/groups/512098985483106/

- https://www.faceBook.com/groups/426282137432533/

- https://www.faceBook.com/groups/kindle.goodreads/

- https://www.faceBook.com/groups/eBooksBooksPromo/

- https://www.faceBook.com/groups/192635697552276/

- https://www.faceBook.com/groups/kindle.deals/

- https://www.faceBook.com/groups/332043700233334/

- https://www.faceBook.com/groups/books45/

- https://www.faceBook.com/groups/320356974732142/

- https://www.faceBook.com/groups/bookjunkiepromotions/

- https://www.faceBook.com/groups/BookPromotion/

- https://www.faceBook.com/groups/2204546223/

Next, if this is not enough you can search for groups that do Tweet exchanges. These are authors that tweet for each other.

Free website submissions

There are literally hundreds of websites where you can post your free promotion. Most of them will require that you do this 1 or 2 weeks before your actual free promotion starts.

Note that there are gigs on fiverr who propose to do this for you, but I've never tried these myself, so I cannot say if this is a reliable option or not.

Ok. Here it goes:

For starters, here is a list of sites where you can submit the announcement for your book for free. I have to put immediately some reservations on this list, because these sites are changing continuously. Some switch from free to paid submissions. Some will direct you to another site. At the time of writing this list was correct. I keep a more accurate and up-to-date list available on my site on this page : Free eBook Promotion Websites

- BargaineBookhunter.com
- IndieBookoftheDay.com
- AuthorMarketingClub.com
- Frugal-Freebies.com
- YourDailyeBooks.com
- AwesomeGang.com
- FreeDiscountedBooks.com
- FreeBookDude.com
- TheFussyLibrarian.com
- EReaderPerks.com
- BookGoodies.com
- FreeeBooksDaily.com
- BookCanyon.com
- IndieBookPromo.com
- ItsWriteNow.com
- FreeeBooksBlog.com
- FreeBooks.com
- PixelofInk.com
- KindleMojo.com
- eBookDealoftheDay.co.uk
- eBooksHabit.com
- TheEReaderCafe.com
- OneHundredFreeBooks.com
- FreeDigitalReads.com
- iLoveeBooks.com
- MommaSaysRead.com
- JungleDealsandSteals.com
- eBookDealoftheDay.com
- EReaderNewsToday.com
- DigitalBookToday.com
- PixelScroll.com
- SlashedReads.com

- FreeBooksy.com
- AddictedtoeBooks.com
- BookGoodiesKids.com
- FreeBooksHub.com
- EverythingBooksandAuthors.com
- eBooklister.net
- ZoeysonlineBooks.com
- BookAngel.co.uk
- IgniteYourBook.com
- BesteBooksFree.com
- ClickReading.com
- Daily-Free-eBooks.com
- PeoplesReads.com
- Contentmo.com
- BookFreebies.com
- FictionHideaway.com
- Hunt4Freebies.com
- Ereadergirl.com
- GreatBooksGreatDeals.com
- KindleNationDaily.com
- Super-E-Books.com

There are some other sites, like Authormarketingclub that link directly to other free submission sites. And of course, some of these sites will propose to do all this work for you, for $20 or $30 .

You could also use some software, like iMacro or Selenium in which you create a scenario to fill out all these forms. To create such a macro needs some time to figure out how to do it and is out of the scope of this book. But once you have done it, for all following submissions for your next book, you just change the data that you want to enter and you execute the macro again to fill this data on all these websites.

Your website

Blog: For your website, and if you run a blog, you should write a blog post. You can include a description of the book and maybe some samples. At this stage, you will just announce "Coming soon". If you already have your cover ready you should include that in your blog post.

Landing page: You can create a landing page just for your book that you will use for PPC advertising if you're going to do that.

My Books: If you have several books, you could include a separate "My Books" page on your site, which appears in the main menu.

Sidebar: If you use a sidebar, you can use that to show a smaller image of your latest book. With something like "Coming soon". If you have several books you could use a rotator plug-in, which shows your books one after the other. There are paid and free rotator plug-ins. Search for rotator in the Wordpress plug-in directory.

Other

Press releases: You can write a press release for your book and send it to dedicated press release sites. Here are some:

- http://www.onlineprnews.com/

- http://www.prlog.org/

- http://www.free-press-release.com/

- http://www.24-7pressrelease.com/

- http://www.1888pressrelease.com/

- http://www.pr.com/

- http://www.i-newswire.com/

- http://newbookjournal.com/

Goodreads.com: This is the biggest community of authors and readers. You can create a profile, list your books and promote them.

Mail your list: If you have a decent list, then you could send out a broadcast message, announcing your free promotion period. Some authors prefer not to do this, and send only a message to announce a special Countdown deal. If you have a huge list, then you should definitely use this in the post-launch period, when your book is really for sale.

Forums: Depending on the topic of your book, you should consider to participate in forums on your topic. However, it is better to use forums to educate yourself, rather than for promoting your book.

Signature: You could also include your book title or a link to your book in the signature of your emails.

Update your books: If you already have other books, this might be the right moment to check if you should maybe update or improve them. Because a free promotion period will also draw people to your other books.

Launch day

The magic day is there. You have polished your book, uploaded the latest and greatest version and today your promotion starts. Now you have done already most of the work. But you should give it a final push, now that your book is actually available for a free download.

For Facebook and Twitter, repeat the same steps as you did during the prelaunch, but now you announce that your book is actually available for a FREE download. If you use a site like Hootsuite, this will now be just pressing one button to send out all your Facebook, Twitter and Google+ messages.

Free book websites

If you have gone through the free website submission list that I mentioned in the prelaunch phase, you may have noticed that some sites will only permit to you to announce a book when it is actually available for free when you post the submission. You will have to go those sites to announce now that your book is available NOW for free. Here are some of these sites:

- http://www.besteBooksworld.com/

- http://www.dailycheapreads.com/

- http://snickslist.com/

- www.daily-free-eBooks.com

Paid promotions

According to the Amazon T&C's for the Amazon Associates Program, you may NOT use any PPC campaign to drive traffic directly to Amazon, using your affiliate links. Here is the extract from the Amazon site:

> **"Prohibited Paid Search Placement"** means an advertisement that you purchased through bidding on keywords, search terms, or other identifiers (including Proprietary Terms) or other participation in keyword auctions. **"Proprietary Term"** means keywords, search terms, or other identifiers that include the word "amazon," "Kindle," "myhabit," or "Javari," or any other trademark of Amazon or its affiliates (see a non-exhaustive list of our trademarks), or variations or misspellings of any of those words (e.g., "ammazon," "amaozn," "kindel," and "javary"). **"Redirecting Link"** means a link that sends users indirectly to the Amazon Site via an intermediate site or webpage and without requiring the user to click on a link or take some other affirmative action on that intermediate site or webpage. **"Search Engine"** means Google, Yahoo, Bing, or any other search engine, portal, sponsored advertising service, or other search or referral service, or any site that participates in any of their respective networks."

So, if you want to do PPC campaigns for your books, you have two choices:

1. Send the traffic directly to Amazon, but NOT using your Amazon affiliate link.

2. Send the traffic to your own site, and send them than through to Amazon using an Amazon affiliate link. You can NOT use an automatic redirect for this. Visitors have to click on a link to get from your site to Amazon.

Facebook promotion

If you are going to do some paid promotion, one of the things you can do is, to promote the post that you have posted on your personal page or your Fan page. To do that, click on the Promote button. On a post that you make on your personal page, you will see that button right under the post.

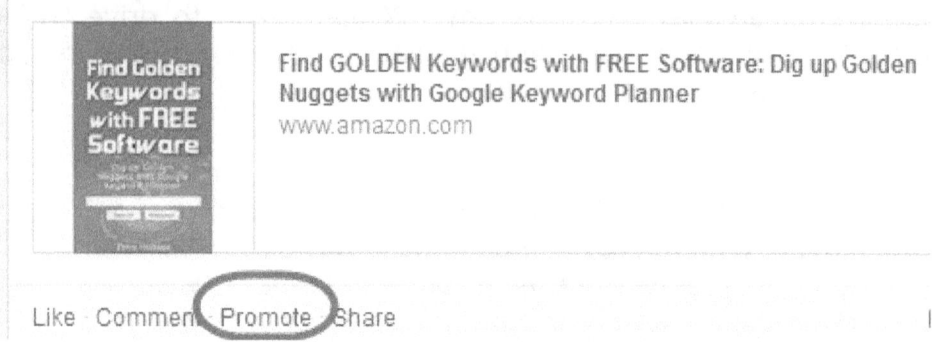

On a Fan Page, you see that button on the right hand top side of the page.

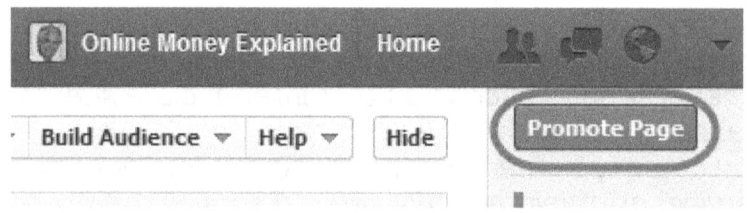

You can now fill in the parameters for your target audience and your budget. For a couple of dollars this can result in lots of downloads.

You can of course also setup a "classic'" PPC campaign on Facebook.

https://www.faceBook.com/advertising

Other sites for paid promotion

There are a number of other sites where you can do paid promotions. Here is a list:

- https://ads.twitter.com

- https://www.goodreads.com/advertisers

- https://www.stumbleupon.com/ads

- http://indie.kindlenationdaily.com/

- http://www.bookgorilla.com/advertise

- http://www.worldliterarycafe.com/content/homepage-featured-author-sponsorships

- http://www.booklybooks.com/authors/

- http://digitalbooktoday.com/3-dbt-social-media-buzz-package

-     http://www.freeBookdude.com/p/advertise-with-free-book-dude.html

- http://www.thekindleBookreview.net/advertise-books/

- http://www.booktweetingservice.com/

- http://thefrugalereader.com/promotional-opportunities/

- http://bestindieBooks.com/great-indie-books/submit-book/

- http://www.kboards.blogspot.fr/p/authors.html

- https://www.bookbub.com/partners/pricing

- http://yourbookauthors.com/20-2/welcome/authors/

- http://freeBooksy.com/for-the-authors/

- http://digireaderlounge.com/author-promotion

- http://www.freeBookshub.com/authors/

- http://www.freeeBooksdaily.com/

-           http://authormarketingclub.com/members/wp-content/plugins/oiopub-direct/purchase.php?do=banner

- http://www.whowrotewhat.net/advert.html

- http://www.pixelofink.com/authors-corner/

- http://indiepromotor.com/

- http://bargainbooksy.com/sell-more-books/

- http://www.iloveeBooks.com/advertising.html

Post launch period

Now your book is launched. Can you now sit back and relax? Sure, that's something you can do. But by far the BEST thing you can do is: Start writing your next book!

By far the most effective thing you can do to increase your income, is by writing more books. How many? There is no golden figure for that. But if you publish 10 books they will look like any Top 10. There will be 4 or 5 at the bottom that will do a little bit or nothing. Then there will be 2 or 3 that are making reasonable sales. And you may have 1 or 2 that really sell very well.

This whole book business is a matter of write, publish and repeat.

But besides starting your next book, there are a couple of things that you would do on a regular basis, like checking your sales data, sales rank en reviews.

Reviews

When I wrote this book, I hesitated if I would include a chapter on reviews. Yes, reviews are important. And I could have ended this chapter with: Just wait for your reviews to come in. Because that's more or less all that is allowed by Amazon when it comes to getting reviews. Here is the official version of Amazon, what is **NOT** allowed:

> *"Promotional content:*
> *• Advertisements, promotional material or repeated posts that make the same point excessively*
> *• Sentiments by or on behalf of a person or company* **with a financial interest in the product** *or a directly competing product (including reviews by publishers, manufacturers, or third-party merchants selling the product)*

- Reviews written **for any form of compensation** other than a free copy of the product. This includes reviews that are a part of a paid publicity package
- **Solicitations for helpful votes**

Inappropriate content:
- **Other people's material** (this includes excessive quoting)
- Phone numbers, postal mailing addresses, and URLs external to Amazon.com
- Videos with watermarks
- Comments on other reviews visible on the page (because page visibility is subject to change without notice)
- Foreign language content

We have a **zero tolerance policy** for any review designed to mislead or manipulate customers.

If you have a direct or indirect financial interest in a product, or perceived to have a close personal relationship with its author or artist, we'll likely remove your review.

Here are a few examples of reviews that we don't allow:

-A product manufacturer posts a review of their own product, posing as an unbiased shopper.

-A shopper, unhappy with her purchase, posts multiple negative reviews for the same product.

-A customer posts a review in exchange for $5.

-a family member of the product creator posts a five-star customer review to help boost sales.

-A shopper posts a review of the product, after being promised a refund in exchange.

-A seller posts negative reviews on his competitor's product

-An artist posts a positive review on a peer's album in exchange for receiving a positive review from them"

Well, I think that summarizes it pretty well.

Any form of asking for a review, or obtaining a review in exchange for something is forbidden. The only thing that is allowed is asking for a review (and not a positive or helpful review) in exchange for the free book that the customer is reading.

When you browse regularly books and reviews, and you follow blogs and forums you start to get an eye for fake reviews (called 'shills') and practices that people use to get them.

Now if I can spot them, then I think that Amazon can spot them to. So if you use any of these practices, it is on your own risk. Ask yourself the question if it's worth it to get 5 positive reviews for your 10th book, if that may jeopardize your account or even lead to an account termination.

Just to be complete, I list here a couple of practices that I'm aware of. Notice that I haven't used any of these myself, so I cannot comment on the fact if they work or not.

List of No-No's

• Reviews posted by friends or family

• Review swaps (falls under compensation)

• Fake reviews from the author, posted under another name

• Even worse: fake reviews on competitor books

• One step further: reviews on competitor books and adding "I think that this other book from author X is better"

• The ultimate no-no: buying book reviews. I don't know what the sanction will be from Amazon if they discover this, but I think it will be severe. If you want a good read on the topic, here is one from the New York Times. It dates from August 2012, but maybe things have changed in the meantime.

• Paying people to buy your books. This is the extreme ultimate no-no. The first time I read about this I asked myself: What's the point? I mean, you buy your book for $10 and you will get $7 back in royalties from Amazon. But of course the 'trick' here is, to get your book boosted up on the sales ladder. And then hoping that the positive financial effect of all this will finally outweigh your 'investment'. Well, again. I think (but I cannot prove it) that Amazon has things in place to detect shady practices like this.

I leave it as an exercise to the reader to imagine what will happen to your reputation if you use an extremely black hat tactic like this one and it gets discovered and published publicly.

But aren't there any other ways to get reviews, other than just waiting for them? Yes, there are. There are book review websites . See the next chapter. One other way is, to solicit an Amazon reviewer.

Amazon reviewers are people who do Amazon reviews as a hobby. They are not paid for the reviews. But they take it very seriously. So if you want an honest review , try to find an Amazon reviewer. As stated, these people will give your book an honest and realistic review. So be prepared for a 2 or 3 star rating if you send them a 'get-rich-quick' book of 20 pages, or some other book of which you know already deep in your heart, that it will not withstand any real critical review.

It would go way too far to explain in detail all the ins and outs of the Amazon reviewers culture, but you better try to understand how this community works, before soliciting a reviewer. An excellent book on his topic is "How to Get Good Reviews on Amazon: A Guide for Independent Authors & Sellers", by Theo Rogers. I would highly recommend any author to read this book.

How to find an Amazon reviewer for your book? Look at books in the same niche as your book, and go through the reviews. And see if any of the reviews are made by an Amazon reviewer. You can find a ranking of all reviewers here. http://www.amazon.com/review/top-reviewers

The AuthorMarketingClub has a tool that can find these reviewers for you (you have to become a member to use it).

The only advice I would like to give: Play it by the rules and respect the Amazon T&C's.

Some other questions about reviews that you may be asking yourself. (Answers from Amazon)

Who can write Amazon.com customer reviews?

Anyone registered as an Amazon.com customer and who has made at least 1 purchase for ANY product is entitled to write customer reviews.

Does the reviewer have to buy the item from Amazon.com?

No. It doesn't matter where an item was purchased, or if it was a gift, or if the reviewer just borrowed it for a weekend. If someone feels moved to write a review of an item, and they are a registered Amazon.com customer, they are welcome.

I also wrote a book about Amazon reviews which you can find here :

Amazon reviews exposed. the truth about amazon reviews

Book review websites

There are a couple of sites where you can publish your book and people will read them and give a review. You can then use these reviews in the front matter of your book or in the book description. Note that if you give exclusivity to Amazon for your book, you should do all this BEFORE you submit your book to Amazon.

Because if you give exclusivity to Amazon, you may not give away your book on ANY other site. (See the chapter on KDP Select). So don't forget to take these down as soon as you publish.

- https://readersfavorite.com/

- http://www.stepbystepselfpublishing.net/reviewer-list.html . On this (long) list you will see all kinds of sites that publish reviews of books.

- https://www.faceBook.com/groups/reviewseekers/

- http://www.booklistonline.com/

- http://www.goodreads.com

Personally, I only would use sites where people will really read your book and give you a FREE review. I would refrain from any paid reviews, but that is up to you to decide.

Take it as a business (not as a hobby)

Some authors write a book, publish it, and then they are surprised that it doesn't sell hundreds of copies a day. Even after that they did some of the marketing activities as mentioned in this book.

Selling books and getting results is a business. Like any other business. Ask yourself the question: What action(s) would I undertake, now that I have put $10.000 into creating my book?

I think you would do 80% or 90% of all that is possible to make your book(s) sell. It's not because writing and publishing a book costs almost nothing, that you shouldn't put all efforts in to sell it.

Experiment with changes

When you have published your book, you should analyze your sales results. And from the reporting data that you get from Amazon, you can learn a lot:

- You don't get enough clicks on your affiliate links. Check the sources where you have put those links.

- You get clicks on your links to your book, but people don't look at the detail page (=they don't click on your book to see the details). This may indicate that there is something wrong with your presentation. Either the description, the title/subtitle or your cover or all of them.

- You get raving reviews, but not enough. This means that the people who have read your book like it, but people cannot find your book. Verify your keywords and categories. It may also mean that you don't ask for a review in your book. There is nothing wrong with asking readers, at the end of your book, for a review.

- In general, experiment with changes. But, like with any A/B or split testing, only make ONE change at the time. If you change AND the cover AND the description AND the title you don't know exactly what made the change in your sales results (if any).

Outsourcing

When you start to write more and more books, you will quickly notice that you don't have time to do everything yourself anymore.

Formatting your books, site submissions, online marketing activities.

Now most of these activities are very well defined. This means that they are easy to outsource. For example, when you have created your complete submission file with all the information, you can now easily outsource that, by sending the submission file and the list of free submission sites to someone who is going to do that for you.

You can try to find someone on a freelance site. However, I think it is better to search for someone that you trust and to whom you can outsource other tasks also. Like formatting your books, the whole process of cover creation, the whole publishing process on Amazon, all marketing activities etc.

That's what's called a Virtual Assistant (VA). You can find people that propose themselves as a VA on freelance sites like freelance.com or odesk.

Write a series

As I already pointed out, the best thing you can do, is write more books. Even better is, to write a series of books that are related to each other. If you write fiction, writing a series is easier than with non-fiction.

For non-fiction, if you have a book that sells really well, you can think of publishing a more complete version. Which you will sell of course for a premium price. So you could sell the "basic" version of 100 pages for $3.99 and the "Ultimate" version of 200 pages for $5.99.

You also can create bundles. You can think about this if you have enough books out there. Let's say at least 10. I wouldn't use any bestsellers (if you have any) to use in a bundle. Take 3 books. One that sells ok, one that sells average and one that sells a few copies.

Calculate the total sales price for these 3 books and take 20% or 30% off. This is now an interesting deal for your customers and you sell a bit more books.

Your book doesn't sky rocket right from the start? Don't despair. There is no hurry. It is not like selling paper books in a traditional bookstore. Your book will not disappear from the shelves if it doesn't sell 100 copies the first month.

Actually, with online sales there are completely different sales patterns for books. A book may be online for months and then suddenly sales start to explode. We call that a breakout.

Here are four sales patterns:

The hidden book: This is a book that has a more or less horizontal graph with low level daily sales. This is a book that just sits there and no one can find it. Not necessarily a bad book, but it will never break out. This can be caused by one or more of the following: bad cover, no good story, bad category choice, priced too high.

The boiler book: This book sells steadily a couple of books a day. From time to time there is a small spike. It behaves like a kettle on a stove. It has potential and it bubbles. This is a good candidate to become a breakout. But that can take weeks, or months before that happens.

The marathon book: This one builds up sales slowly over time. This is a sign that it is a good book. It gets good reviews. On a certain moment in time word-of-mouth will do the rest and it will turn into a breakout.

The breakout: These are, by definition, good books. On a certain moment in time, they quickly climb up the sales ladder. 10, 50, 100, 1000 copies a day. This is also boosted by the "also bought" algorithms. Reasons for a breakout can be all kinds of things: It gets promoted in a television show, it gets a raving review on a big blog, it's about a topic that suddenly comes hot in the actual news etc. Notice that a book may be a boiler book for months, selling a couple of books a day and then suddenly turn into a breakout.

Some authors worry about the fact that their books or parts of it may be copied, used in blogs etc. But should you really worry about this?

First of all, a lot of people that copy books, software and other digital products would never have bought it anyway. Not even for $0.99. So these are not lost sales.

Second, I've been long enough in IT (Information Technology) to confirm that no protection mechanism can protect your product for 100%. It's just a matter of time and effort. If a hacker/pirate really wants to get some product for free, and he knows enough about security and protection mechanisms, he will find the point of failure.

Also, look at it this way: This book talks a lot about making your book known by using free promotions. So, if someone copies your book and gives it to a friend, look at it as free promotion instead of an illegal copy.

Also don't forget that there are thousands if not hundreds of thousands of people interested in your book. If you're selling 100 books a day, for months if not years, should you really worry about the handful illegal copies that are circulating around?

Having said that, there are a couple of things you can do to prevent copying or at a minimum, inform you of illegal copies so that you can take some action if the thing really gets out of hand.

Google alerts: You can setup some Google alerts. Take 2, 3 or 4 sentences out of your book of which you are sure that they are unique (Just put them into Google search and see if that sentence is already published somewhere). Then, setup 3 or 4 Google alerts with these sentences. When someone uses the exact same phrases in an article you will get an alert in your mail box. Not foolproof but it helps a bit.

DRM: When you submit your book to Amazon, you will be asked if you want to use DRM or not. DRM stands for Digital Rights Management. When you apply this to your book, readers cannot simply copy and paste text from your book into another program.

Having said that, DRM is a protection mechanism which is not 100% foolproof. For obvious reasons, I will not go into further details of this in this book.

Boost your downloads.

There are a number of things you can do to further boost your sales and downloads. Here are some of them.

Find fellow writers

Competition is a good thing in any business. And in the book publishing business there are enough readers to satisfy all GOOD authors. So don't consider all authors in your category as competitors. Rather try to see them as fellow writers. If you can create a good relationship with these writers you both can benefit from it.

You may read each other's books and give real constructive feedback. And if it is for sale, your fellow writer may give you a real, sincere and honest review.

WSO

If your book is in the marketing space, you may consider running a WSO (Warrior Special Offer). This is a special offer on the Warrior Forum. This is the biggest forum about online marketing on the internet.

JV partners

Find Joint Venture Partners (JV Partners). These are people that may be willing to promote your book to their list or help you in other ways with your promotion. You can find JV partners either through your contacts or on forums like the Warrior Forum or Digital Point.

Your email list

One of the best ways to promote your book is to use your list. You have a much closer relation with the people on your list than through any other media. Of course, if you have a list of 100 subscribers, this will not make a huge difference in your sales (if any). However, if you have a list of 10000+ subscribers, using that list will be the BEST way to boost your sales. By far.

Promote your retailer

I'm not sure if this is really going to impact your sales, but promoting your retailer with some good publicity on your blog, may give your sales a small punch. On the other hand...

Never criticize your retailer

It sounds obvious, but if you publish your book on Amazon and you write either in your book, or on your blog criticism about Amazon, they may not appreciate it, if you have a large following.

Be patient

One of the other things you can do to not get to nervous about your sales results is... Being patient. I've seen too many comments on forums like:"I published my book last week and I only have made 4 sales". Book publishing is a long term activity. Wait 2-4 months at least to make a conclusion if your book is selling or not. You cannot tell from the first 3 days.

Category hopping

As I explained in very long detail about categories, when your book starts climbing up the sales ladder, it will automatically move up to the higher categories. This is all automatic. You don't have to do anything about this.

However, you may see after a while, by observing competing books, that you haven't put your book in the right categories. Some people recommend to contact Amazon to request for a change, but things are much simpler. If you detect that your book should be better in another category, just go to the submission page on your Amazon bookshelf.

Now you can change the two categories where your book is listed in. You can also update the keywords which will modify the search terms in which your book will appear.

If these changes still don't have the desired result that your book appears onto the Amazon site under category XYZ instead of ABC, then the only solution is to contact support and explaining that you think that your book is better categorized under XYZ then under ABC.

This is called category hopping. If your book cannot break through the top 100 barrier, see if there isn't a less competitive category. But that still fits your book!!!

Use YouTube

You can create a 1 minute video trailer for your book on YouTube. Video attracts lots of people. And making a video is not rocket science. You can use Windows Movie Maker to make a simple presentation just with a couple of images. Make sure that you have the copyright to use them. Or you can create a PowerPoint presentation and record it with recording software like Jing or Camtasia. Don't forget to put the proper tracking code for that source in the link, so that you can measure how much traffic and how many sales you made from this media.

Use Slideshare

If you have made a PowerPoint presentation you can put it up also on Slideshare. This is a rather popular site where people put up presentations just about anything. Again, I cannot confirm that it will generate droves of leads, but all bits can help.

Viral Marketing

This is a dream for many marketers. Unfortunately, there is no "secret formula" that explains how to create something that goes viral. It just happens.

Going viral means: You publish something somewhere. Because it is funny/engaging/touching a couple of people will send it to their friends. These friends will send it to their friends. People will start to 'like' it on Facebook. And this can go VERY fast. Within a couple of days THOUSANDS of people will look at your article/video/blog or whatever. If you can score something that goes viral, that will impact your sales for sure.

What kinds of things have potential to go viral? Funny pictures and videos. Videos about things that touch people in their heart: love, divorce, war, hunger.

I'm 100% sure that if you do EVERYTHING in this book, your sales will be more than if you do NOTHING of all the things that I wrote about. How much? 10%? 50%? 100%? More?

Of course I cannot tell. This depends first of all on...... Your book!! The subject, the cover, the contents etc.

Take a couple of the ideas from my book and implement them. Then see what works and what doesn't. A couple of weeks later try some other things. And see how these work.

Marketing anything is a lot about trial and error. But don't give up when you have tried a couple of things and they don't give the results you expected. Take a couple of other and try again.

What's next?

Ok. Your book is online. Now, what's next? Go on holidays? Write your next book? Hanging onto your screen 24 hours a day to watch your next sale coming in? '

There are a lot of things that you can do in this post-publishing timeframe. That's what this chapter is all about.

Tracking sales and other data

"Scientia potentia est". This Latin phrase was written in 1597 and means "Knowledge is power". When you have published your book, and you have put in all those efforts which I described before, you now should track a couple of things.

• Your sales. That one is obvious.

• The sales rank of your book(s)

• Your author rank

• Your reviews

• The efforts that are giving results, against the things that you did but that aren't doing anything.

Tracking your sales

This one is obvious. You should track the sales of your book(s) on a daily basis. Amazon will give you every day the number of copies sold and the number of copies borrowed. On Amazon you will get nice charts about this, but only for the last 90 days. I strongly suggest to download this data and keep it for future analysis. At a minimum, you should record every day the following:

• Number of sales per title

• Number of borrows

• Sales Rank of your book in its category (or categories)

• Number of reviews

In addition, you can keep track of your Author Sales Rank, although that only becomes really interesting when you start to get into the top 100 listings in the main categories.

Also record every month all the reports that you get from Amazon. You can download all these reports and put them into a spreadsheet to analyze your data.

This will give you detailed insight and can give you clues to questions as: Where does my traffic come from? How many clicks did I get on each book? How many sales did these clicks generate? And much more. Again "knowledge is power", so keep these reports stored in a safe location. On an external disk and a backup copy somewhere on internet.

Sales rank in categories

When you have published your book and you haven't made a sale yet, you will see something like this under your book.

Language: English

ASIN: B00JXYM9V2

Text-to-Speech: Not enabled ⊻

X-Ray: Not Enabled ⊻

Lending: Not Enabled

No sales data at all

Would you like to **give feedback on images** or **tell us about a lower price**?

After the first sale, you will see something like this.

Text-to-Speech: Enabled ⊻

X-Ray: Not Enabled ⊻

Lending: Not Enabled

Amazon Best Sellers Rank: #654,274 Paid in Kindle Store (See Top 100 Paid in Kindle Store)

Would you like to **give feedback on images** or **tell us about a lower price**?

The book has a rating called the "Amazon Best Sellers Rank". I will explain further on in this book with much more detail what the Amazon Best Sellers Rank is.

And a while later, you may see some additional lines come up, like this:

Amazon Best Sellers Rank: #143,279 Paid in Kindle Store (See Top 100 Paid in Kindle Store)
#20 in Kindle Store > Kindle eBooks > Reference > Writing, Research & Publishing Guides > Editing
#60 in Kindle Store > Kindle eBooks > Business & Money > Skills > **Business Writing**
#65 in Books > Reference > Writing, Research & Publishing Guides > Writing > Editing

These numbers (20, 60, 65) are the individual category rankings.

ALL categories and subcategories have their own ranking list. From N°1 to N°X in which X is the lowest ranked book. Ratings in a category will only be displayed if they are in the top 100.

So, if your book is rated on N° 120 in a category, you will not see a line like that under your book, because it is not yet in the top 100.

This also explains why sometimes you will see such a line, and the next day it's gone. This means that you've went from into the top 100 to a lower place.

Now what is the meaning of the following?

#20 Reference > Kindle eBooks, Writing, Research & Publishing > Editing

This is the Main category "Reference" in which there is a subcategory "Writing..." in which there is a subcategory "Editing". (I left out the Kindle Store > Kindle eBooks part, because that just means the top category of the Kindle eBooks store under which ALL eBooks are organized).

Any book starts in the lowest category where it was submitted. In this example Editing. After a while the book gets into the top 100 in that category. And let's say that it gets to number 20.

One level higher up, the category "Writing, Research & Publishing Guides" has its own ranking in which are listed ALL books in ALL categories that are listed under that category. One of them being "Editing".

Now on a certain moment the book is going to enter also that top 100. For example on N°50. This number is of course always higher (=lower ranking) than the category below it.

In a similar way, after a while, when it gets high enough up in the category "Writing, Research & Publishing Guides", it will enter the top 100 in the category one level up. The category "Reference". And let's say that it ends up there on N°80.

And finally, when the book really explodes, it gets into the top 100 of the next level up "Kindle eBooks". But let's say that that is not the case yet for this book and it is on N° 300 in that highest category.

So we have:

Editing: rank 20

Writing, Research and Publishing: rank 50

Reference: rank 80

Kindle eBooks: rank 300.

This will end up on Amazon as a rank 20, as shown in the image above.

In other words, the rank within a category that is displayed is always the rank that the book has in the lowest category **that is shown**.

How can you find out the rank of that book on the other, higher level categories? The only way is to click on that category and see where the book ranks. If you don't see it in the top 100, it means that its rank is lower than 100.

After a while, and if the book sells, it will get to N°1 in the lowest category "Editing". At that moment, the same line on Amazon will show:

#1   Kindle   eBooks>Reference>Writing,   Research   & Publishing>Editing

And it will remain like that. Because when the book climbs up in the higher categories, it still will be shown as the line above. Until it reaches the N° 1 position in the category one level higher. So in this example, when the book hits N°1 in Writing, Research & Publishing, it will be reported by Amazon as

#1 Kindle eBooks>Reference>Writing, Research & Publishing

This is of course a bit of marketing from Amazons' side. Because it just shows better to display

#1 Kindle eBooks>Reference>Writing, Research & Publishing>Editing

rather than

#50 Kindle eBooks>Reference>Writing, Research & Publishing

The second line in the example

Amazon Best Sellers Rank: #143,279 Paid in Kindle Store (See Top 100 Paid in Kindle Store)
#20 in Kindle Store > Kindle eBooks > Reference > Writing, Research & Publishing Guides > Editing
#60 in Kindle Store > Kindle eBooks > Business & Money > Skills > **Business Writing**
#65 in Books > Reference > Writing, Research & Publishing Guides > Writing > Editing

is exactly the same reasoning, but in a completely different main category and subcategory with its own rankings. So, this book is on N°60 in the lowest category "Business Writing". I cannot tell from this line how it scores in the higher level categories (Skills etc.)

Finally the 3rd line is the rating in the Kindle Book Store. This book store doesn't have the same categories as the Kindle eBook store. It contains all eBooks AND the hardcopy books.

Note that all these ranking figures may change, even if the book doesn't sell a single copy for a while. Normally, its ranking will go down, because the other books will sell. But if this book sells one copy and competing books in the same category sell more, the ranking of this book will go down.

In the same way, if this book sells some copies and the competition also, the ranking may not change for this book, despite its sales.

Finally, these figures are calculated on sales made over a certain period. So suppose that this book has recently made 4 sales and the book just above 5 sales. But the last sale was a couple of days or weeks ago. When the reporting window slides more forward in time, the book just above will "lose" a sale, in the reporting window. So its ranking will drop and the ranking of the book just beneath it will improve. Even without selling one copy.

To resume, the category ranking will not show you how many sales it made, but how its sales perform, compared to the others.

Free downloads are completely separated from paid downloads. So, you should imagine two completely different stores. One with paid books and the other one with free books. Free books have their own rankings. These rankings show up when you browse the free eBook store. Everything you see concerning a book under the "Amazon best sellers rank" on Amazon, concerns only real sales. No free downloads.

However, if you select the best sellers list on Amazon, you will see two tabs. One for paid books and one for free books.

Hot releases

On the right hand top side of your screen you see the "hot new releases" books. Which books appear in that display? Books that are recently released and that are climbing fast. Notice that even 1 or 2 sales are enough to gain a lot of places and to make it in the "hot new releases" section.

Here is an example:

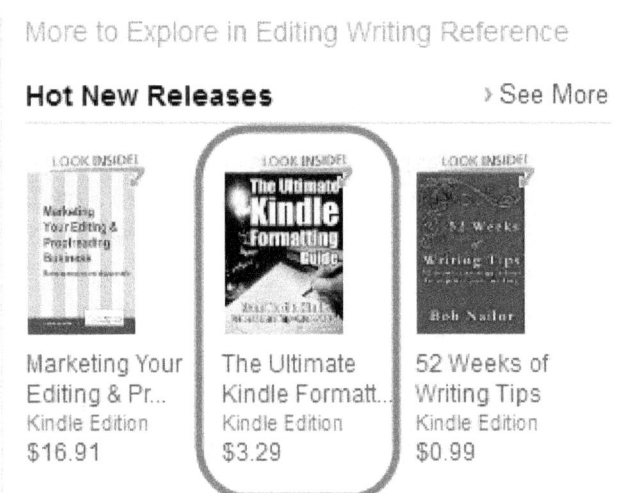

Hot New Releases ⟩ See More

Marketing Your Editing & Pr...
Kindle Edition
$16.91

The Ultimate Kindle Formatt...
Kindle Edition
$3.29

52 Weeks of Writing Tips
Kindle Edition
$0.99

I launched this book, and it sold a couple of copies the first day. After 1 day it was in the hot release section.

Does that really boost your sales? Well, it depends in what category you made some major progress. If it is in the lowest subcategory then there is only a small fraction of visitors who will see your book in that section.

If your book appears in the same section, but now on a main category page, a lot more eyeballs will see it, so the effect will be MUCH more significant.

The also bought list

Just under your book description appears the "Customers who bought this item also bought" section. Why does this list appear here and not some other list like "movers & shakers" or "What other items do customers buy after viewing this item" (which you find all the way at the bottom under your book)?

Simply because that list has much more influence on a potential buyer than all the others. Again, nothing on Amazon is just "hazard". If something appears on a specific location on a page (above the fold, on the left or the right etc.) there is a reason for that.

Now what items are listed in this "Customers who bought..." queue? Notice that there are scroll left and right buttons for this list and that there are 99 items maximum in this queue. But which ones? And what determines their order?

That's another well kept secret from Amazon. It appears that not just the sales of these books determine their ranking in this list. But also some 'promotion' factor. That's where the sophisticated algorithms from Amazon kick in.

Suppose that two books A and B in this list have approximately the same number of sales but B just a bit more. Book A is sitting on an uphill curve and will likely sell more and more. Book B is sitting on a downhill curve. Has reached already his high and is selling less and less.

Which one would you promote if you were Amazon? Right. Book A. So in the algorithm from Amazon there is some predictive analysis involved. And probably some other factors.

It is clear that when Amazon puts that sticker 'to promote' on your book, that will influence your sales.

Author Rank

Your author rank is calculated using sales that you made overall and within each subcategory. Author rank will show up on the detail page of a book in the "More about the author section". The number will only show up if it is in the top 100 overall, or in the top 100 of a browse category. Here is an example of the author rank of a successful writer, Jonathan Stone.

Amazon Author Rank beta (What's this?)
#4 Overall (See top 100 authors)
    #1 in Kindle eBooks > Mystery, Thriller & Suspense > **Thrillers**
    #1 in Books > Mystery, Thriller & Suspense > **Mystery**
    #1 in Kindle eBooks > Mystery, Thriller & Suspense > **Mystery**
    #2 in Books > Mystery, Thriller & Suspense > **Thrillers**
    #2 in Books > **Literature & Fiction**

The same information will also be shown on your author page.

As an author you can see your own rank on your Author Central page under Rank.

Author Rank beta (What's This?)

Notice that the Author rank is calculated over all your books in a category. And one figure for your overall rating taking into account ALL categories. This means that if you have published 1 book and you have reached a reasonable Author rank of let's say 30 in a category, when you publish your next book, your overall author rank will nosedive.

Because now your rating will take into account this second book which is still sitting on the bottom of the ladder.

The more books you write, the smaller this dip will be. Because if you have a good author rank with 10 books, when you publish book 11 it will only weigh in your author rank for a small part.

Amazon Best Seller Rank

This is probably one of the figures that is the least understood. Before I try to explain how this number is calculated, let me repeat what I said in my disclaimer at the beginning of this book. In the calculation of this number there are a lot of factors that are taken into account:

• Your current and most recent sales

• Your past sales

• The sales rate of your book. (=How many sales in a certain period)

• The total period that they have been for sale (The publication date)

And probably a whole lot more. And all these factors weigh in for a certain amount in the overall calculation of your Amazon Best Sellers Rank.

What does Amazon themselves say about Author Best Sellers Rank?

> *"While the Amazon Best Sellers list is a good indicator of how well a product is selling overall, it doesn't always indicate how well an item is selling among other similar items. Category and subcategory best seller lists were created to highlight an item's rank in the categories or subcategories where it really stands out.*
>
> *We choose a few of the most popular subcategories in which the item has a high ranking in relation to other items in that subcategory, and showcase the item's rank on the product page. As with the main Amazon Best Sellers list, these category rankings are based on Amazon.com sales and are updated hourly."*

Well, that doesn't tell us much HOW they really calculate that number.

The sales rank is calculated hourly, but the data that is taken into account is over the last 24 hours. Recent sales weigh in more, and historical data weighs in less.

Do I know the exact formula? No. Does anybody know? Probably some Amazon employees. Anyway, I've never seen an article or blog post or help page showing the exact formula. But this is the same discussion as "How does Google rate their pages". It is known that they use over 200 parameters to calculate a Page Rank. But no one seems to know the exact formula. I once wrote a funny article on my blog about this. You can read it here: The Secret Google Algorithm Finally Revealed!

But in such a case, you can use the black box approach. Feed something in and see what comes out. And because there are thousands of authors writing about their sales rank and sales, you can than draw some conclusions about what probably is going on behind the scenes.

So here are a number of findings:

Relationship between sales and overall sales rank.

By analyzing the figures of authors, their sales and their sales rank (and of course your own figures), you can get some ballpark figures, how sales influence your sales rank.

Sales Rank	Daily Sales
1 to 5	4000+
5 to 20	3000-4000
20-35	2000-3000
35-200	500-2000
200-400	250-500
400-500	175-250
500-750	120-175
750-1500	100-120
1500-3000	70-100
3000-5000	25-70
5000-10000	15-25
10000-20000	10-15
20000-50000	2-5
50000-100000	1

The higher you get in this table, the more sales are involved and the more reliable the figures. And vice versa. So for a book on the bottom of this table, it may sell one day 1 copy, the next day 2 and the next day 0.

When your book is in the 50.000+ range, the sales rank will vary wildly. One day it may rank on 200.000 and the next day on 300.000 or 100.000. This simply means that the sales are insignificant from your book AND competing books in that range. Your book sells 1 copy and your competitors none: Your sales rank may bump up 100.000 or more. And vice versa. Your book doesn't sell one copy on a certain day, and a competitor book sells 1 copy, your sales rank may go down with 100.000.

Conclusion: As long as you're on the bottom of this list, don't worry too much about your sales rank. Wait till you get to the 100 sales a day mark (if you ever get there), and then things start to be much more reliable and interesting.

Only real sales are taken into account. Free downloads don't influence your Sales Rank.

Because your sales rank is relative to sales from other books in your category, it also means that if due to some external factor everybody in your category starts to sell more, the rise in sales rank may not be as spectacular as you would have expected by just looking at the sales.

Amazon also uses some predictive sales analysis to forecast where your future sales will go. This explains why a newly released book can be ranked higher than a book that was released a year ago. Even when the other book has more total sales. Amazon can predict that this new released book will overtake the 'older' book using the sales rate.

However, while your book climbs up the sales ladder, the competition will get tougher. Because the other books have loads of historical sales data. That's why breaking through the 10.000 barrier is difficult and breaking through the 5000 barrier is even more difficult.

A marketing effort may create a spike in your sales rank. However, if after a couple of days your sales slow down, the historical data from your competitors will start to weigh in more and more, and your sales rank will go down quickly. That's why it is better to space out your marketing efforts, to maintain a steady sales rank.

When are you a "bestselling" author?

Notice that the sales rank on Amazon is called "Amazon Best Sellers Rank" and not "Amazon Bestsellers Rank". The wording is maybe not the most appropriate because the "Amazon Best Sellers Rank" is just a number from 1 to over a million. So, any book on Amazon that has sold at least one copy will have a "Best Sellers Rank".

Now if you're in a low competition category like "History Books>18th Century", just a couple of sales can boost you to the top in THAT subcategory. So, you will see something like:

#1 Kindle eBooks>History>18th Century.

Does that make you a bestseller author? Well, it depends on your definition of bestseller. For most people, a 'bestselling' author sells hundreds if not thousands of books a day. But if it flatters your ego, you can make a screenshot of your #1 rating in 18th century books, and post it on your blog. :)

Your book is a failure. Now what?

What is a failure? Does it mean that your book is bad? No not necessarily. But other books are perceived as better. Or they are just marketed better. Or easier to find.

Ok. You have published your book, gave it your best shot, gave away thousands of free downloads, posted it on lots of free websites, announced it on your website etc. etc. and.... it still doesn't sell. For weeks or months.

Should you despair and start looking for a rope? No, of course not. It just means that you joined the biggest authors group on Amazon. Welcome to the club.

Now what? Should you give up and go and search for a job at Mc Donalds? No, of course not. If you want to succeed in your writing career than you have to accept that some of your books will not fly.

And maybe your first book was just one of those unfortunate ones. The best remedy is, to write another book. And another. And you will see that the quality WILL improve. You will write better and better. And sooner or later one (or more) of these books WILL sell.

Maybe not thousands a day. But imagine that, on the long term, you have 15 books out there and half of them sell 10 copies a day. That's about 70 or 80 a day in total. Which is roughly around $4000/month.

Yes, it may take you a year or two to get there. But nobody said it was easy.

So, only advice I can give: KEEP WRITING!!

Your book is a success. Now what?

Great! You have launched your book and it sells 10 copies the first day, 50 copies a day after a week and 100 copies a day after a month. Congratulations!

You have made it. Your book sells like hotcakes. Should you start shopping for a suit for your upcoming interview by Oprah Winfrey?

Ehhh, cool down. And stay humble. Success is relative. First of all, if you sell 100 copies a day, yes, you will have a very comfortable income. But don't forget that amongst the REAL bestsellers, who are selling THOUSANDS of books a day you're still a beginner. But you already can be very satisfied with your success.

Now what? Can you sit back and just see the money roll in every month? Well, you can take some time off and go on a nice holiday. You deserved it.

But now that you've got there in a top rank, you have to make sure to stay there!

Watch your sales rank. When you see a significant change downwards, you should do everything to keep your ranking. Lower the price of your book; throw in a Countdown deal or a free promotion. Read the books that are threatening your position and that are climbing up the ladder fast. (For this, watch the "Movers & Shakers List" in the category where you rank).

But the best you can do, as I already wrote on several places: Write another book! You already have hard proof now that you can write a good book. So why not write an even better one that is going to be on the NY bestsellers list. And this new book may even drive sales of your other book through the roof.

So I conclude this chapter with the same advice as the previous one. Whatever your success on Amazon: KEEP WRITING!

Distribute your book through affiliates

A couple of words about selling your book through affiliates. Now I'm not talking about other people that may promote your book on Amazon. Because that will be an ignorable portion of your sales on Amazon (if any).

No, I'm talking about selling your book through an affiliate network like Clickbank.

Now let's see what that implies. First, when you are going to sell your book through that channel, you cannot make it exclusive anymore on Amazon. So no more access to KDP select.

Second, you have to put in place a complete backend for your affiliates if you want them to promote it. A professional sales page, promotion material like banners, covers etc.

Third, you have to make it attractive for affiliates to sell YOUR product instead of another.

So the first problem you will run into is a pricing problem. Suppose that you have been successfully selling your book on Amazon for $3.99 and now you want to go for the affiliate road on Clickbank. Do you think that affiliates will be interested to promote your book for a VERY high commission of 90% which is a mind blowing $3.59? No.

Now I have found a book that is selling both on Amazon and on Clickbank. The retail price for this eBook on Clickbank is $47 and the affiliate commission is $25. So the author gets $22.

The price on Amazon, for the same book in hardcopy is $35.

See the problem? This book has a sales rank of 900.000+. No surprise there. How many people are buying hardcopy books for $35? VERY few.

So in this case, being on Amazon or not doesn't really make any difference. Because 0 x $35=0.

Now would there be any pricing strategy to sell through both platforms? No. not really. Why? Because to sell any book in reasonable volume on Amazon, it should be priced less than $9.99. How to figure that out, besides common sense? Just look at the top 100 in a couple of categories and see how these books are priced.

Only VERY few are priced above $10.

Now how much should you give to an affiliate to make it interesting for him to sell your book? Even if you give away the whole $10, you won't find an army of affiliates.

Conclusion: If you're going for the affiliate road, just forget any sales through any other publishing platform.

Ok. Now what is going to follow is pure speculation. And in a real case you would have to do some real market research to figure out your pricing strategy.

But let's take a hypothetical case. You have a book which sells really well on Amazon for 3.99. Let's say 100 copies a day. That's roughly $200 a day or $6000 a month income.

Now you have this idea of moving it to Clickbank. As pointed out, your sales will disappear from Amazon. Now suppose that you want to make it interesting for affiliates to sell your book. You put aside $25 a sale for your affiliate.

You want to make some money also yourself. Let's say a real minimum of $4.99 so that the book stays under the psychological limit of $30.

Now to make the same income as you had before on Amazon, your affiliates would have to sell 6000/5=1200 copies a month.

Feasible? Yes, if you have some big affiliate marketers going for it with big email lists this is not at all impossible.

But there is a 2nd VERY important difference by doing it this way. For all these sales, you will also pick up the email of the buyers. They are not on your list yet, because they haven't opted in. And some marketers just don't use double opt-in. As soon as they have an email they start their promotion. (Watch out for being classified as a spammer)

But even if you could get only 10% of these 1200/month on your list, that's 1440 a year, you have added a lot of value to your list.

Now this book is not about affiliate marketing or how to build a list. But it is clear that selling your eBook on Amazon or other publishing platforms is not the ONLY way to sell a book.

But don't forget, if you have a good sales rank on Amazon, and you are going to try something else with your book elsewhere just to 'see if it flies', your sales rank on Amazon will go down fast and you will have to restart from zero if you come back later.

So think twice before you pull a successful book from Amazon for another experiment.

Improve your production speed

If you write a lot, it is obvious that your production speed can have a significant impact on your total production time. Therefore I include here to tips:

Tip 1: If you are still typing with 2 or 3 fingers, take a fast writing course. There are numerous books and sites that will teach you how to learn fast typing. Imagine that you could crank up your speed from 2000 words a day to 8000 or more. Here are some goods books that I can recommend:

- Writing FAST: How to Write Anything with Lightning Speed

- Write Fast: 21 Powerful Ways to Cut Your Writing Time in Half

Tip 2: Use speech recognition software like Dragon Naturally Speaking . Now you just talk into a microphone and the computer spits out the text. If you can talk fast, you can produce fast. And it doesn't cost an arm and a leg. Prices I saw are from $99 onwards but you can probably find it cheaper.

Keep Writing!

Well, we have come the end of this book. I hope you learned some useful things. I really enjoyed writing this book. And if I may give you one more time my advice: "KEEP WRITING!".

Thank you

Thank you for having read my book till the end. I hope you liked it and that you have learned what you were looking for.

If you have appreciated my book I would like to ask you just ONE favor. Please leave me an honest review on Amazon by going here

If you got this book for free during a promotion period, I would highly appreciate it if you could leave me an honest review. Please click on the following link

Yes, I'll give you a review.

It will only take you a minute or two. I value any feedback from you. If it is really positive, I have attained my objective of adding real value in my book for you. If it is average or less, I can use your feedback to make it better. So, click here and give me your opinion. I thank you in advance.

I wish you lots of success in your online activities.

Timo

About the Author

Biography

Timo is a writer, blogger and IT expert. He writes about complex things, like keyword research, affiliate marketing and online marketing. But in a language that is understandable for everybody.

He uses 30+ years experience in computers, networking, hardware, software, development, internet, marketing, sales and online business to teach others how to grasp complex issues. His international experience, working abroad in several European countries, US and Africa has given him a broad view on different cultures and civilizations.

He has followed the development of the internet right from the start. In the 80's just with email and private networks, and from the early 90's onwards he was one of the first ones to work with the first websites.

Learn from the author how to setup an online business, how to understand everything about search engines, how to create your own   'internet   life-style'.

His books are extremely results-oriented: You are looking for a solution to a specific problem? When you read a book from the author, you will find the answer.

In straight-to-the-point explanations without the fluff.

When Timo is not writing or blogging he spends his time on the magnificent beaches between St Tropez and Monaco, relaxing in a pub in Cannes, playing chess or travelling to his home country: The Netherlands.

All Books from the Author

Here are all my books:

- <u>150 Ways to Make Money Online.</u> Learn How to Make Hard Cash with Your Computer from Home

- <u>Find Golden Keywords with FREE software.</u> Dig up Golden Nuggets with Google Keyword Planner.

- <u>The Ultimate Kindle Formatting Guide</u>. From Word to Kindle. Better Formatting = More Sales

- <u>How to Make Money with eBooks. The Best Collection of Marketing Tactics to Boost Your Sales.</u>

- <u>Amazon Reviews Exposed. The Truth about Amazon Reviews.</u>

- <u>The Complete Book Cover Creation Guide. What makes a good cover and how to create your own for FREE</u>.

- <u>How to Make Book Covers that Sell. Everything You Need to Know About Book Cover Design. (Part I of The Complete Book Cover Creation Guide).</u>

- <u>How to Create Professional Book Covers. Make Your Own Free Book Covers Free With GIMP. (Part II of The Complete Book Cover Creation Guide)</u>

Disclaimer

This product is not legal or accounting advice. The author has made all efforts to be as accurate as possible. Due to the continuously changing nature of the internet, some references mentioned in this book may change and may not work anymore. The author shall not be liable for any loss incurred as a consequence of the use and application of any information presented in this book.

The author has no control over the content, nature and availability of the websites mentioned in this book. References to these sites do not imply a recommendation or endorsement by the author.

While every attempt has been made to check and verify the information in this book, the author does not assume any responsibility for errors, omissions or contrary interpretation of the subject matter herein.

Earning claims mentioned anywhere in this product are completely dependent on the time and effort invested, and are in no way guaranteed.

The author and the affiliates of this book are not liable for any damages or losses associated with the content of this book.